Frenemies

Frenemies

What to do
when
friends
turn mean

Hayley DiMarco

Revell

a division of Baker Publishing Group
Grand Rapids, Michigan

Published by Revell
a division of Baker Publishing Group
P.O. Box 6287, Grand Rapids, MI 49516-6287
www.revellbooks.com

Printed in the United States of America

Library of Congress Cataloging-in-Publication Data
DiMarco, Hayley.
      Frenemies : what to do when friends turn mean / Hayley DiMarco.
        p.   cm.
      ISBN 978-0-8007-3304-9 (pbk.)
        1. Teenage girls—Religious life. 2. Female friendship—Religious as-
pects—Christianity. 3. Enemies (Persons)—Religious aspects—Christianity.
I. Title.
      BV4551.3.D55 2010
      248.8′33—dc22   2009044973

Published in association with Yates & Yates, LLP, Literary Agents, Orange,
California.

Creative direction by Hungry Planet

Interior design and illustrations by Michael J. Williams

10   11   12   13   14   15   16   7   6   5   4   3   2   1

Contents

Introduction

WHAT IS A FRENEMY?

> If an enemy had insulted me, then I could bear it. If someone who hated me had attacked me, then I could hide from him. But it is you, my equal, my best friend, one I knew so well! We used to talk to each other in complete confidence and walk into God's house with the festival crowds.
>
> Psalm 55:12–14

The frenemy. She's a friend and an enemy. A little bit of good and a little bit of bad. She's nice a lot of the time, but boy, when she's mean, she is oh-so mean. How did it get this way? When did she turn? And now what do you do?

Living with a frenemy is difficult, if not risky business. She can attack you on a whim and then love you just as fast. You like being with her, most of the time, but sometimes she makes you sick to your stomach and tired to the bone. The frenemy isn't easily understood or changed. Her ways need some explaining, but more than that, your reaction to her ways needs a boost. She's chosen her path of destruction, and now it's up to you whether you will capsize in the storm of her mean or change your course and maybe even help her to correct hers.

So what makes a frenemy any different from an enemy? And should they be treated just the same, or should the friend part of the relationship make a difference? Good questions, both. First let's take a look at the definition of *enemy* in order to get a better idea. According to *Merriam-Webster's Collegiate Dictionary*, an enemy is "one that is antagonistic to another; especially: one seeking to injure, overthrow, or confound an opponent." Have you ever felt like the opponent of your frenemy? It's so weird how someone can claim to love you, can spend time with you, and can even publicly profess their "like" for you, yet at the same time can be looking for opportunities to hurt you or mess with you all the time.

We've covered the definition of an enemy; now let's try look at the definition of a friend. A friend is defined as "one attached to another by affection or esteem." The biggest difference here being the presence of affection and esteem. Seems like a reasonable definition.

Okay, now let's mush those two defs together for our own definition. "Frenemy: someone attached to another by affection or esteem who seeks to injure, overthrow, or confound them as an opponent." That's a mixed-up puppy. "I love you," "I hate you," "I love you, but I hate you." Ugh! Not a good feeling for either person involved. Frenemies are at the very least confused and

friend + enemy = Frenemy

more than likely divided. It's *frenemy = friend who acts like an enemy* hard to have an opinion or to take a stand on something like friendship when you are forever changing the definition of it. In the *mean girl = enemy* book of Proverbs we read that, "A friend always loves, and a brother is born to share trouble" (Proverbs 17:17). A friend should be constantly loving, constantly on your side, but the frenemy is anything but consistent—consistently inconsistent is more like it.

A lot of times the frenemy is actually worse than the full-on enemy. In my book *Mean Girls: Facing Your Beauty Turned Beast*, I wrote about this full-on enemy— the Mean Girl who is anything but a friend. The Mean Girl is one of the ultimate tests of girlhood, but how you deal with her is hugely different from how you have to deal with your frenemy. Your frenemy is a part of your life; she isn't going anywhere soon, and you have to decide if you're going to try to salvage the friendship or just walk away completely.

The subtle difference between the Mean Girl and the frenemy is that the frenemy was invited into your life by you or is there because she's related to you. You love her, or at least like her, and because of that your reactions to her are probably gonna be different than your reactions to a Mean Girl. It's complicated, life with a frenemy—much more complicated than dealing with a Mean Girl who isn't your friend at all. Just like a Mean Girl, your frenemy might make you sick, tired, or even depressed, but more than a Mean Girl ever could, your frenemy is probably affecting your spiritual life. ~~please men~~ *please God*

The real problem with the frenemy, though, isn't how she makes you feel; that is a good signal that something is wrong, but it's only a symptom. The real problem is her influence on your spirit. In whatever way she takes your eyes off of God and makes you focus on worry, fear, anger, loneliness, depression, or anything else that leads you to question God or sin, she has drawn your spirit away from the pursuit of holiness and into the pursuit of acceptance. In every situation you have to ask yourself, "Am I now trying to win the approval of men, or of God? Or am I trying to please men? If I were still trying to please men, I would not be a servant of Christ" (Galatians 1:10 NIV).

You can't go on not knowing when she's going to hug you or hurt you. You can't go on being afraid of the one you love. Something needs to be done, and it needs to be done now. That's why you have to agree to be honest with yourself and, most of all, to be willing to do what it takes spiritually to improve the situation. My favorite question I like to ask people is this: if you keep doing what you're doing, you'll keep getting what you've got—is that enough? If it's not and you want change, then you've come to the right place.

Now, I have to say before we go any further that no friend is perfect. No one is so consistently loving that they never hurt you or leave you wondering what just happened. Human nature makes us hurt each another accidentally and sometimes purpose-fully, but that doesn't make us all frenemies; just fallen. Nope, the frenemy is a particular kinda mean. She pulls you in with her kindness and attention, and then she smacks ya down with her hidden or even blatant insults and jabs. Repeatedly! She doesn't even have to be 50–50 nice and mean. A friend who's mean to you even 20 percent of the time is still a major frenemy, because that means one out of five times you talk to her, she's going to leave you hurt and abused. And that leaves you off balance, never sure who she's gonna be next.

You need to ask yourself a lot of questions about your friend to figure out if you're dealing with a real frenemy or just a normal, everyday, run-of-the-mill human who makes mistakes and gets a little moody. And that's what we're gonna to do in this book. It's time to decide once and for all if this relationship is worth it or if it's time to chuck it. And if you can't chuck it, you've gotta learn how to deal. Life is short and you don't need a friend who treats you more like her enemy than her loved one. But when is enough enough? Ready to find out? Good.

Before we dive in, though, let me point out just one little thing that you might never have thought about: Jesus himself, the perfect man, the one everyone should have been glad to have as a friend and afraid to turn into an enemy, had his own frenemy to deal with. His name was Judas Iscariot. He spent months on end with Jesus. They worked together, they ate together, they laughed together, and they probably even cried together. But Judas wasn't all friend all the time. He had other ideas of what he wanted out of the relationship.

Jesus was a popular guy. Everyone wanted to be with him, but he couldn't possibly travel with and befriend every person who wanted his time, so he picked out twelve men. These twelve guys would enter his inner circle as friends and disciples. They would leave their friends and families and travel with Jesus to serve him, learn from him, and love him. Judas was one of these lucky guys. He was given the job of treasurer, the handler of the money. That meant that when any member of the group wanted to eat or to buy some clothes or anything at all, they'd have to go to Judas to get the cash they needed. It was a very important position, to say the least. But, of course, Judas proved himself anything but trustworthy. While Judas and Jesus worked together, Judas didn't pull anything; he was a friend to Jesus. But one night that all changed, and when it did, this is what happened, "Jesus was deeply troubled. He declared, 'I can guarantee this truth: One of you is going to betray me!'" (John 13:21). This betrayal would send Jesus to his ultimate sacrifice. And the fact that it was his friend Judas who would start things must have been disappointing to the Savior (see Matthew 26:48–50).

You're not alone when it comes to frenemy problems. You have someone who understands more than you could ever know. He watched his friend stab him in the back in the worst possible way, and ultimately this friend would kill himself from the guilt of doing what he did. Yes, Jesus knows what it is like to be loved and hated by the same person. So as we start to look into God's Word, remember that you aren't alone. Others the world over are going through just what you are going through, and the Savior himself is intimately aware of your pain. You're not alone, my friend.

One last thing before we dive into diagnosing and healing your frenemy problem: Let me suggest a way to make this book sink deeper into your heart, and that is through music. When I read a book on deep matters of the spirit, I like to turn on my own soundtrack of life that drives me to the place I want to be mentally and spiritually as I listen and learn, seeking God's face and his truth. My favorite worship music is my continual soundtrack while I write and read anything about God. The words lift up my heart and my mind to where they need to be and help me get my spirit ready for the things I am reading. So give it a shot: pick up your iPod, download some tracks if you are without, and turn 'em on. Then, read on about God's desire for you and your frenemy!

> Friends can destroy one another, but a loving friend can stick closer than family.
>
> Proverbs 18:24

10 Signs
Your Friend Is a Frenemy

Malicious witnesses testify against me.
They accuse me of crimes I know nothing about.
They repay me evil for good.
I am sick with despair.
Yet when they were ill, I grieved for them.
I denied myself by fasting for them,
but my prayers returned unanswered.
I was sad, as though they were my friends or family,
as if I were grieving for my own mother.
But they are glad now that I am in trouble;
they gleefully join together against me.
I am attacked by people I don't even know;
they slander me constantly.
They mock me and call me names;
they snarl at me.

Psalm 35:11–16 NLT

As long as there have been and will be friendships, there have been and will be problems. We even see it in the Bible: King David's life was torn apart because of friends who wanted to destroy him (1 Samuel 19:9–10; Psalms 41:9; 88:8). How many nights did he lull King Saul to sleep with his music when all of a sudden Saul wanted David killed? David's way of life was ripped away from him; he was all alone, living in a cave, asking God for answers. He didn't understand why the people he loved, prayed for, and grieved for now hated him. But they did, so he begged God for relief.

As David knew all too well, a frenemy can be worse than a full-on enemy because you love her so much. You want her to love you back in the same way, and sometimes she does, but somehow, some way, she always seems to let you down.

But true friendships were made to stand the test of time. Weren't they? After all, the book of Proverbs says that "wounds made by a friend are intended to help, but an enemy's kisses are too much to bear" (Proverbs 27:6). We should be able to fight and make up. No one should have to feel like they're walking on eggshells with their friend. We should be able to point out each other's faults, disagree, and even take a time-out from each other, if necessary. But when the waters get rough, how do we know if we're average, run-of-the-mill friends or if we're frenemies in disguise?

Feelings can't be trusted. But sometimes how you feel about or around your friend can be a signal that something might be going wrong. Real friendship is a good thing. It should give you energy and hope. It should help you to be strong and confident. It should be a safe place, helping you to know that in this big

world, at least one person always has your back. But sometimes friendship can feel anything but good. You disagree, you argue, you storm off. You hang up on each other, you scream, you cry. You want the same thing, but both of you can't have it (or him). But at what point do you say enough is enough? And at what point do you just make up and go to a movie?

Since how you feel about your friend at any given time can change, and since feelings can sometimes stretch the truth, if not totally lie to you, it's a good rule of thumb to have more proof than how you feel to support your claim about a friendship gone bad. If you're a follower of Christ, then you have just what you need to figure this out. You can always ask one question about your relationships to find out if they're what God wants for you or not, and the question is this: does this person distract you and draw you away from God or encourage you to sin? If the answer to that question is yes in any way, then you're dealing with a real frenemy.

If someone who says they are your friend is tearing you down either spiritually, emotionally, or physically, then you're looking at a frenemy. This can happen in all kinds of ways. She might be talking about you behind your back because she's jealous of anything you get that she doesn't have or because she is just mad at you. No matter what the issue, she is someone whose objective isn't your happiness and well-being but her own, at any expense. And that is completely unbiblical. When your friend takes her eyes off of God and his Word and puts them on herself and her needs, it gets really easy for her to turn into a mean friend, and that can give you more than just a little discomfort.

I realize that "Does she distract you from God in any way?" is a big question. In fact, you might not even realize that some things she does distract you from him and lead you to sin. That's why we're going to go through this list of ten signs that your friend is really your frenemy. I gave you a list like this in my book *Mean Girls*, but this list goes into much more depth looking at the source of your trouble with your frenemy. As you read about these signs, look at each one through the light of God's call on your life to be obe-

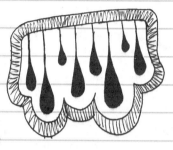

dient to his Word and not to your friend, and also think about your role in the relationship. In other words, are you doing any of these things yourself? It's always important if you're going to be an honest believer—that is, a believer who isn't afraid to face your own sin and mistakes—to see yourself in the mistakes and missteps you whine about in others. One of the first things I say to anyone who is having any kind of relationship problems is that the only person you can change is yourself. No one has the power to make another person think or act the way they want them to. But that's not bad news; it just means that we each have our own lives to live and are only responsible for our own conduct. Sure, you need to figure out if your friend is a frenemy, but please keep one eye on yourself just in case anything in your own heart and life needs correction. That way you will be open and ready to hear the voice of God and make it a living and active force in your life. So, let's take a look at the list and see if you've got any of these things in your friendship.

Sign #1: You Feel Worse after Being with Her

The first and biggest issue in a relationship with a frenemy is that you more than likely feel worse after talking to or being with her. This feeling of discomfort or sadness comes because of her attitude, words, or even actions. The feeling might not be overwhelming; it might be just an underlying and nagging feeling that something just isn't right. Because of that, it can easily be ignored as just another bad day.

I once had a friend point out to me that I got depressed every time I hung out with another one of our friends. It had never occurred to me. I had never put two and two together—my depression and her presence—until this friend pointed it out. After I opened my eyes, I started to see all kinds of ways this person was cutting me down, mocking me, and working to make me feel really bad about who I was. Then I made a change immediately. But until my friend pointed out the connection, I was clueless.

Spotting a frenemy isn't always easy. You get into a groove of friendship and you lull yourself into a sense of well-being, even as things go south. Your friend who once was super nice is now saying mean things at weird times, so you ignore it or write it off as a PMS thing. But it's time to get honest with yourself and figure out if it isn't actually more than a once-a-month occurrence. If you consistently feel

worse after being with your friend, then something isn't right, and it's time to take a closer look.

When I first became a Christian, I had a good friend who wasn't afraid to confront me on issues of sin in my life. And believe me, there was a lot of sin in my life. Each time we were together I would find out one more thing that I was doing wrong. So you would think that when I left her presence I would be bummed, depressed about my inability to get it right, and that I would go home and cry over having a friend who continued to point out all of my faults. But the opposite was true. Each time I left her, I was uplifted and energized because what she was pointing out was truly sin, and sin chains you up, but breaking away from sin sets you free (see Romans 6:18). Each time she pointed out the bad stuff in my life, I was thankful—thankful that she was brave enough to open her mouth and point me in the way of obedience. "The heartfelt counsel of a friend is as sweet as perfume and incense" (Proverbs 27:9 NLT). Friends don't have to be positive with each other all the time. They can and should remind each other of God's law and the faith they both want to have, but they shouldn't be fault finding in order to hurt each other or to build themselves up.

The best way to know if what your friend is saying or doing is godly or just downright mean is to see how her words compare with God's own words. Is she pointing you to him or to her own needs and wants? When she is pointing you to godliness, you shouldn't feel worse after being with her, you should feel better. So check *her* words against *his* and *your* actions or reactions against *his* words as well, and you will know if your friend is being mean or helpful. If your friend is saying things just to make fun of you, insult you, or belittle you, then she's not a friend, she's a frenemy, and what she's doing is mean and unbiblical.

According to God's Word, we are supposed to build each other up, not tear each other down (see Hebrews 3:13), and that's why this type of frenemy is so destructive. She isn't on your side. She isn't fighting the good fight alongside of you. She isn't trustworthy or encouraging; but she encourages your sin of self-doubt, depression, anger, and even disbelief. Blaming God for your life gets really easy when you see this kind of ugliness in the face of a friend. When you can't go to your friends for hope or encouragement, you look at God as if he's dropped the ball. A frenemy distracts you from truth and even tries to help you to sin in all kinds of ways.

Sign #2: She's Overly Defensive

A very important proverb in the life of friends is this: "As iron sharpens iron, so a friend sharpens a friend" (Proverbs 27:17 NLT). Friendship isn't just about feeling good and having fun. It's about that but so much more. Friends should make each other better. That means they can't be afraid to confront each other in the areas where they need confronting. If your friend is sinning, she needs to stop, but if you confront her or ask to talk to her about it and she gets overly defensive, refusing to hear a thing you are saying, then she's got problems. The biggest problem is her refusal to listen to God's Word as it applies to her life.

People get defensive because they're either embarrassed or just plain afraid to confront or hear the truth about themselves. Deep down, they know something is wrong, or at least they fear it. For example, if you accused me of doing crack, there's no way I'd get defensive, because nothing could be further from the truth. But when you accuse me of being a shopaholic, I admit, I can get a little defensive. That's because you've hit close to home on one of my favorite indulgences.

If you wanna be faithful and godly, you have to accept criticism and not fight the people who give it. After all, life isn't about you; it's about God, his glory, and what He wants in or out of your life. If someone is asking you to take a look at a part of your life that is suspicious, your first response should be introspection instead of anger. The frenemy overreacts to anyone's questions about her life because she don't want to be found out.

The trouble with this kind of "friend" is that you can't count on her to sharpen you or trust her to be sharpened herself. She is so preoccupied with how she looks that she has stopped looking at God. She refuses to let the Word of God tell her what to do. Her spirit is shut off, and that means that her heart is too. And out of that comes all kinds of sin—sin that is contagious to you and everyone she spends time with. If your "friend" is overly defensive, then more is going on than your hurt feelings. You always have to look at the spiritual health of the people you call "friend," especially the ones you spend most of your time with. "Birds of a feather flock together" isn't a cliché for nothing. It's true: <u>we tend to become like the people we hang out with.</u> Hang out with someone who's afraid of uncovering and exposing her sin to the people she's closest, and you run the risk of doing the same exact thing. Hang out with transparent people who aren't afraid of anything but looking away from God, and you're surrounded with the possibility of finding tons of hope and strength in friendship with them.

Sign #3: She's Jealous

Let's face it: a lot of girls struggle with jealousy, and out of that comes all kinds of mean. Jealous friends are mean friends. Their focus is on themselves—their needs and wants instead of yours. God makes it clear that we need to love one another and not get jealous or envious of each other's success (see 1 John 4:21 and 1 Peter 2:1). And while that applies to you, it also means that if your friend isn't loving you enough to be happy for your wins, then she's sinning and she may be more frenemy than true friend.

The trouble with this way of thinking is that it can be contagious. Girls who are jealous are usually jealous of more than just one person. So when she's with you, this girl will rant and rave about other people and how much she hates them for what they're getting in life. This is an unhealthy attitude as well as an unhealthy environment for a believer to be in. You have to ask yourself if letting her vent her jealousy on you is keeping your mind and heart on God or on the things of this world. If your friend is jealous much and likes to take it out on you or drag you into her misery, then you have a real frenemy.

Jealousy is your mind's attempt to say that God is unfair. Jesus told a parable about some workers who got mad at the boss who paid everyone the same wage no matter how many hours they worked (see Matthew 20:1–16). He told it to show us that we have no right to be jealous over what others get that's better than what you get. Jealousy leads to destruction. People who claw and fight to be first are gonna end up being last.

Unfortunately, if your friend is jealous of you, you don't have a lot of hope of ever pleasing her or changing her into someone who celebrates with you. And in her refusal to be happy when you're happy, she is denying the very God you serve and love (see Romans 12:15).

Sign #4: She's Controlling

You can't serve two masters (see Matthew 6:24). When a friend controls you (tells you what to do, how to think, how to dress, etc.), bosses you around, and manages your life, she's pretending to be God, and you're letting her. A frenemy is a girl who wants to control all the shots. She doesn't trust God with her life or anyone else's, so she controls everything.

The frenemy will say she isn't controlling, she's just trying to help you, or she knows better than you. And for a while you might just buy it. You want her to like you, you don't want to be mean, and so you go along with everything to keep her happy. But eventually it starts to wear on you. And soon you feel trapped. You've let her have control for so long that it's just the way things are now, so how will you get out? Control isn't a characteristic of a healthy friendship. In fact, it's the exact opposite. It's a sign of slavery—"I'm the boss and you're the slave, so you do what I say, period, the end." That's not how friends treat each other. Control should never be a part of friendship.

This frenemy leads you to sin when she insists that you give up your responsibility to not be controlled by anyone but God himself. "Don't you know that when you offer yourselves to someone to obey him as slaves, you are slaves to the one whom you obey?" (Romans 6:16 NIV). When you obey her, you become her slave. If you're a slave to her, you're no longer being obedient to God. It's one way or the other, and you and you alone have to choose.

In Scripture, the only thing a believer is charged with controlling is herself (see 2 Peter 1:5–7). So when you step outside of that will of God and let someone control you, you've lost control of yourself, the one person you are charged with controlling. As a believer, you can't let that happen. A friend who tries to control you is more enemy than friend.

Sign #5: It's All about Her

In a lot of relationships, one person talks more than the other. Maybe one is more needy or just more talkative, but in a good relationship both friends get to share their feelings and their thoughts with each other. When the sharing gets lopsided because she hogs the conversation and it's all about her, something's wrong.

Frenemies

Frenemy Control?

Does your frenemy control you? Take the quiz to find out. On a scale of 1 to 10, with 1 being not true and 10 being completely true, rate each of the following statements:

1. I like to do whatever my frenemy asks so she won't get mad. 1 2 3 4 5 6 7 8 9 10
2. I'm trying to get my frenemy to change a lot of things about herself. 1 2 3 4 5 6 7 8 9 10
3. I often cry because of my frenemy or shout at her. 1 2 3 4 5 6 7 8 9 10
4. I think I hate her. 1 2 3 4 5 6 7 8 9 10
5. Sometimes I just want to get even with her. 1 2 3 4 5 6 7 8 9 10

Now add up your score. _____

Scoring:

1–15: You seem to be doing a good job of not letting your frenemy control you. Sure, she's mean, but you handle her attacks calmly and with wisdom. You are on the way to learning how to best help her to see the value of kindness over mean.

16–35: Things could be worse, but they also could be better. More than likely your frenemy is taking advantage of you and you aren't happy about it. She controls more than your feelings, and life wasn't meant to be that way. But don't worry; there is hope. You can make a change today that will help you get back the control you need and maybe even help her to learn to be nice.

36–50: Ugh! Sounds like you're allowing your frenemy to mess up your life. The amount of control she has over you is unhealthy spiritually and emotionally. You need to make some serious changes in your relationship with her, and now is the time. Take advantage of this book to learn how to better handle mean friends and even how to walk away if things just get too out of hand.

Friends turn to frenemies when they are don't really care about you. Their goal is to talk and to be heard. Every trauma is her trauma; yours are insignificant. Every victory has to be her victory because if it was yours, well, then it just wouldn't be that amazing.

These kinds of girls are always changing the subject. You try to talk to her about something important to you, and within one minute she's changed the subject back to her. It goes something like this:

> YOU: I'm really bummed about what Katelyn said the other day. I really wanted her to listen and to understand where I was coming from, but she was so heated, I didn't get to say anything.
>
> FRENEMY: Well, I can't believe Mr. Timmons gave me a C on that test. Who does he think he is? I'm gonna do something about this!

And the conversation stays on the topic of her, never getting back to you. In your desire to be involved in her things, to listen and to care, you just interact with her stories and let yours drop off the radar.

I have to say that I've known a lot of girls who act like this. They're oblivious to the fact that they never listen and always change the conversation back to themselves. And each time I find one like that, I move on. I don't have the time to sit and listen to her rehearse the misery in her life without ever looking up long enough to see the others around her. God's plan isn't for us as brothers and sisters in Christ to focus inward, always obsessed with what we are feeling. A girl who does this has lost touch with the reality of who God is and what role she plays in his world. She has walked away from serving him and serves only herself. And that's a dangerous place to be.

This friend can be tragic because her disinterest in you can lead you to all kinds of self-doubt and isolation. We're called to fellowship with each other (see Hebrews 10:25), and that means that we share our fears, our hopes, and our faith back and forth. It doesn't mean you silently nod in agreement as one of his kids complains when she should be praising or obsesses over anything other than God. This kind of girl can derail not only your heart but also your faith.

Sign #6: She Never Forgives

The sin of unforgiveness can lead to all kinds of other sins. When someone refuses to forgive, they plant a seed deep in their heart that sprouts all kinds of junk like resentment, bitterness, jealousy, envy, greed, and a lot more. Everything that comes from an unforgiving heart is a rejection of God and his commands (see Matthew 6:14–15; Mark 7:22–23) that forbid things like resentment, bitterness, jealousy, and greed.

If you have a friend who holds onto unforgiveness like her favorite teddy bear, then you're probably living with a really angry frenemy. And if she can't forgive you for something, then chances are you're feeling hurt and even betrayed. A lot of times when you don't get forgiveness from a friend you start to feel guilty, as if their unforgiveness is your punishment for what you have done wrong. But God has a way to deal with mistakes. When you mess up, all you have to do is go to God and confess that what you did was wrong. That apology is then followed with His forgiveness. "If we confess our sins, he forgives them and cleanses us from everything we've done wrong" (1 John 1:9). When a person can't forgive someone who has apologized for what they did, then that person is essentially saying that their standards are higher than God's because they require more than just a confession.

The girl who refuses to forgive is refusing to obey God, and when she does, she drags you down into a cycle of punishment and fear (see 1 John 4:18) and worry about satisfying the conditions of an irrational human being. Your focus then moves from God to the wishes of a crazy woman. If you start to believe her accusations, you can easily start to punish yourself as well, by doing things that prove to yourself just how bad you are, as if you have to stand in agreement with her judgment. This is a spiritually unhealthy place to be. As children of God, we are supposed to go to each another with our disagreements and problems and then work them out (see Matthew 18:15). Don't let the unforgiving friend pull you down into her spiritually unhealthy pit.

Sign #7: She Encourages You to Sin

A friend who does this might not seem like a frenemy. She can come across really nice and seem to always have your back. If you need her to lie for you, she'll back you up no matter what you ask. Want to get out of work today? She'll help you come

Frenemies

Numbing yourself with idols

When your life is stressed and you look for comfort, escape, or hope in something other than God, you run the risk of making that thing or person a substitute for God. And that's called idolatry. Making idols isn't just something they did in the olden days. It's happening right now and right here. As a follower of Christ, you can't let anything or anyone take God's place. Take a look at God's Word and see for yourself how dangerous the sin of finding comfort outside of God can be.

(Check out: Exodus 20:4 and Ephesians 5:5)

up with a good excuse. Want to return a dress you wore one time and get your money back? She'll drive you to the store. Yep, on the surface she seems like a super good friend, but if you look deeper into the spiritual health of your relationship, you'll find an unhealthy alliance: each of you helping each other to disobey God's law.

It's never an act of kindness or love for any human being to encourage, or even to put up with, a friend's sinful choices. Basically you're enabling her to look into the eyes of God and reject him, deciding to do whatever feels good or right at the time. Maybe you've been trying to ignore this sign that your friend is your frenemy because paying attention to the sign means realizing that her support of your choices is sinful for *both* of you. The problem is no longer the evil frenemy but *you* and your use of your frenemy for sinful gain.

Sometimes frenemies don't literally help you to sin, but in a less obvious way their actions help you to choose sin. In other words, she's violent, hateful, or bossy, so in your mind you sin by thinking of ways to get her back or to hurt her. She does something mean, and that makes you look to something sinful for relief. You eat to find comfort, instead of going to God with your worries. You stop eating to have something you can control, instead of letting God be God and trusting that that's enough. You cut, you hate yourself—whatever it might be, it's a sin that is fed by her meanness toward you. That doesn't make what you do justifiable, but it does make her friendship destructive. No one should drive you to sin because of their meanness. No one. This frenemy is leading you down a path of desolation and separation from the one Being in this world who will never leave you and never forsake you (see Hebrews 13:5). Don't let this girl be the one who leads you away from true love.

But some frenemies aren't such unsuspecting participants. A lot of them don't *help* you sin but they *encourage* you to sin. This kind of girl convinces you that getting even with someone who hurts you is your only option. She's the one who brings you all the best gossip and shares it with you to your heart's content. She's the one who convinces you that you absolutely have to have that $150 pair of shoes

because nothing else will go with that dress. And, she's the one who asks you to do something against the rules in order to help her out. She distracts you from what really matters and points you away from God's will and His law.

The signs that you have this kind of frenemy are a little more obvious than others. She seems bent on revolution. She wants to fight everyone and everything, and she wants you

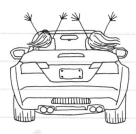

to be her sidekick. She's Thelma and she's looking for a Louise. God makes a special point of condemning these kinds of people when he says it is not a good thing to be the one who leads another into sin (Matthew 18:6–7). But if you know God's Word and still go in willingly to help her, you have no excuse, either. You have to stop the cycle of obedience to her whims and start to say yes to righteousness instead of sinfulness.

Sign #8: She Loves to Talk about Other People

"A gossip separates the closest of friends." ~ Proverbs 16:28

Let's face it: gossip's fun. When you can talk about someone, you examine their weaknesses and mistakes, and you feel exhilarated. That's why this sign of a frenemy is probably the hardest one to spot. For girls, talking is how we bond. We become closer and closer the more we talk to each other. And when she comes to you with some juicy news about someone, it's almost impossible to refuse the info. Believe me, I know what I'm talking about. It took me a long time to learn how to stop gossip in its tracks. I wanted to know so badly what the person had to tell me. I wanted to know so badly, it made my mouth water. But I had to make a decision: what was more important—my need for the excitement of some good G, or obedience to God's Word no matter how much I would miss out on? I chose the the missing out part and did what I could to stop the cycle of gossip in my life.

When a girl wants to talk about other people, one thing is sure: she has no moral code on gossip, or at least doesn't stick to the one she claims to have. That means that talking about people is fair game for her. And so that means that your life is fair game too. So when she's away from you and with someone else she wants to bond with, you and your personal life are going to be discussed. Her mouth is flapping as much when she's away from you as when she's with you. That's because a habit is a hard thing to break. She might not be a bad girl deep down; she's just built habits of speech that are unbiblical. And once you create a habit, it's hard to notice it, let alone change it. She might not even know how bad she's hurting you or the others she talks about, but that doesn't make it any less painful or any less of a mistake for you to join in with her.

The frenemy who gossips needs you and your ears in order to stay a frenemy. And that makes doing something about this frenemy a real challenge, but it's one that can be taken on successfully if you choose to keep God's law at the front of your mind at all times.

Sign #9: She Loves Revenge

"Vengeance is mine," declares the Lord (Deuteronomy 32:35 NRSV). That means that revenge, and everything that goes along with it, is God's. It's his thing, and when you take revenge, you take something from God. Thief!—Ugh! Say it isn't so.

The friend who loves to get revenge is really a frenemy, because her need to get back at people is a disaster waiting to

Frenemies

happen. Revenge is never a good idea. Not only is it spiritual suicide, but it leads to all kinds of troubles: fighting, hate, more attacks, stress, worry, punishment, and the list goes on. Revenge feels really good. It feels "fair." Getting even for something someone else did seems like your spiritual attempt to balance sin out—make things right when others do something wrong by doing something wrong back. But God's people are never supposed to do God's job.

When you have a frenemy that gets revenge, you probably are feeding off her passion for "fairness" and want revenge yourself. She is a bad example and a bad influence on a girl who wants to walk with God, not steal from him. Her revenge might seem harmless to you; after all, she doesn't get revenge on you, just on bad people. But that doesn't excuse your acceptance of her sin. And what's to say you won't be next? When a girl is good at taking matters into her own hands then she doesn't draw the line at friendship. She lives to make things even above anything else. And that means that it's just a matter of time before you'll be on her revenge list. This kind of hot-tempered girl is a danger to strangers and friends.

Sign #10: She Loves This World

Anyone who rejects God and chooses to live by the world's ideas of right and wrong is an enemy of God. This is according to God's own words: "You unfaithful people! Don't you know that love for this [evil] world is hatred toward God? Whoever wants to be a friend of this world is an enemy of God" (James 4:4). Does that mean that if your friend is a nonbeliever, she's a frenemy? Well, that all depends on your relationship.

We can't and we shouldn't hide away from the world. Paul puts it like this:

> In my letter to you I told you not to associate with people who continue to commit sexual sins. I didn't tell you that you could not have any contact with unbelievers who commit sexual sins, are greedy, are dishonest, or worship false gods. If that were the case, you would have to leave this world. Now, what I meant was that you should not associate with anyone who bears the name of brother or sister who is sexually immoral or greedy, or is an idolater, reviler, drunkard, or robber. Do not even eat with such a one.
>
> 1 Corinthians 5:9–11

To avoid unbelievers is unbiblical. You can't because you wouldn't be able to be salt to the world. It would be hiding your little light under a bushel. And you shouldn't do it. But with that in mind, do you believe that you can be a best friends with a nonbeliever? Do you believe that you can share your heart, your soul, your mind, all your thoughts, and all your hopes with an enemy of God? Sounds harsh, I know, but just hear me out.

We all have to be willing to look at God's law and test our lives with it. You might not be mistaken in making friends with the enemy; after all, that is how we witness to the world. But when you're friends with God's enemy, you have to be careful how much hope and trust you put in her. Friendship with her isn't off-limits. She doesn't have to be dumped just because she doesn't believe in God, but you can't treat her the same as you'd treat a believer—listening to her advice, confessing your sin to her, and hoping she will have your back in times of need. Because she's a nonbeliever, she can't build you up in Christ.

Frenemies

She can't put you back on the road to righteousness when you fall down. She won't encourage you to go to him or to obey him. Why would she? She doesn't even know him. So you have to remember that she isn't capable of being your best or soul sister, until she comes to know Christ the way you do.

The danger with this kind of friend begins when she starts to distract you, even encourage you, to stop looking to God for your needs, your help, and even your salvation. When she can make you start looking elsewhere for all the things that God promises you, then you should consider her a frenemy. You can certainly be friends with nonbelievers, and you should be, but think carefully about what you say to them and do with them so that you don't get pulled away by them. In everything you do with this frenemy, always remember these words: "Can two people walk together without agreeing on the direction?" (Amos 3:3 NLT). Do you agree with the things she wants you to do and say, and more importantly yet, does God? That should always be the test for whether this frenemy should be near you or kept at a distance.

The frenemy can be hard to spot, but deep down you know something is wrong and she's the reason. You can't look at the symptoms of spiritual sickness in your life and turn away from it any longer. It's time to take a step, right now, in the direction of faith. What you do from here on out will affect not only your spiritual life, but hers as well. So what do you do now that you see some problems that you can't continue to sweep under the rug? Do you say something today? Do you just walk away? Do you fight for her soul and pray your knees off, hoping to help her see the error of her ways? Well, those answers are coming—just hang on. We will look at how to deal with her in a biblical way and how to break up with her completely if you have to. So let's take the next step toward reconciliation and see if we can't turn this frenemy back into a friend.

> Do not be a friend of one who has a bad temper, and never keep company with a hothead, or you will learn his ways and set a trap for yourself.
>
> Proverbs 22:24–25

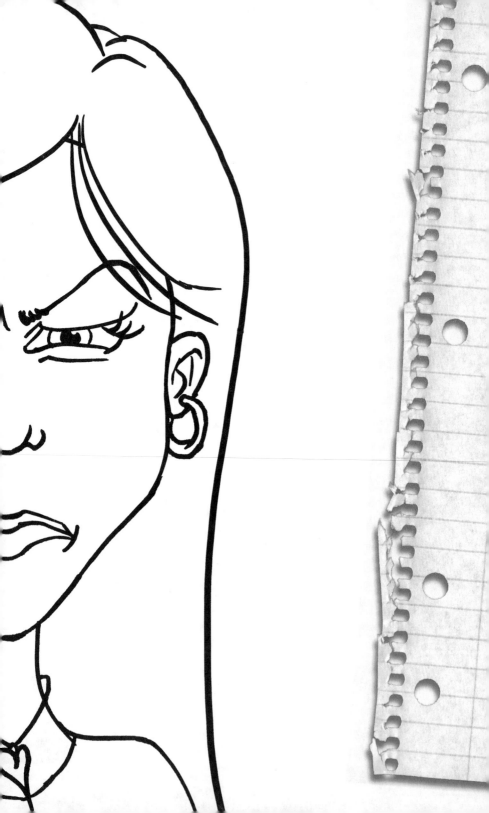

Loving Your Frenemy

> His speech is smoother than butter, but there is war in his heart. His words are more soothing than oil, but they are like swords ready to attack.
>
> Psalm 55:21

Now that we've identified your frenemy, the next step is to answer the question "What now?" What do you do now that you see the problem and want to fix it?

As a believer, you are to have the same reaction to every human being on the planet; you have to love them. Love is a weird thing. It's easily associated with feeling good, even giddy. It seems like an emotion, and one that you certainly can't control. But that isn't true. Love is not just an emotion; it's an action. The reason I know that is because God's Word says it. God calls us to "love our enemies" (see Matthew 5:44). Now, how could he possibly command you to feel lovey and good about someone who hates you? I mean, can God, or anyone else for that matter, command you to *feel* something? Can I command you to feel mushy right now? Go on, do it! Of course not—you can't do it. Feelings can't be commanded. Simple enough.

So when God commands love, he's not commanding you to feel something but to *do* something. And love, as commanded by God, isn't reserved just for family and good friends but is for frenemies as well as full-on enemies. Crazy, huh? So how do you, the friend of a frenemy, love her when she's doing all that she can to make your life miserable? Practically speaking, how do you react to her from now on, and how do you confront her on her areas of sin? We're going to try to answer these important questions.

Relationships are never easy. They require us to use all of God's truths and to believe that when we do, everything will be okay. Things might not look that way on the surface, but underneath, in the center of your soul, things will get better when you obey God's Word no matter what the outcome. So let's take a look at the role of a friend and see if we can't get things back on track.

What Is a Friend?

Most of us think we know what a friend is, or at least we have a sense of it. And I think most would say that a friend is someone who believes in you, who loves you, who cares for you, and who you can trust. But if you have a frenemy, somehow these ideas of what a true friend is have gotten foggy—they've been erased or morphed by a friend who turned friendship on its head when she entered the realm of mean. It's important that you, as a believer, know what a true friend looks like, both so you can fight the good fight against the frenemy and so you can be a true friend yourself. Are you a good friend, according to God's

Word? You need to look at your frenemy and also at yourself as you study the role of friendship in all of your life. So as you read, think not only about her but also about how you can make yourself reflect the image of Christ in your life.

A Friend Gives Her Life for You

According to God's Word, a friend is first and foremost someone who would give their life for you. "The greatest love you can show is to give your life for your friends" (John 15:13). But does that mean that all your friend has to do is take a bullet for you?

If only it was that simple. Kidding! No, I think that this verse gives a lot of insight into the role of a friend in terms of more than just life and death. Think about it from a spiritual perspective instead of a physical one. When someone gives their life for yours, spiritually speaking, they put you first. When you love, that's exactly what you do—you put others first. "Do nothing out of selfish ambition or vain conceit, but in humility consider others better than yourselves. Each of you should look not only to your own interests, but also to the interests of others" (Philippians 2:3–4 NIV).

Now, that doesn't mean you do whatever they want or put their sinful desires first. It means that you put their spirit, their faith, first. You build them up in Christ first. A friend, then, is someone who doesn't fight for her rights, who doesn't hold a grudge, who doesn't boss you around, but who finds ways to serve you rather than herself.

In the Bible it's called dying to self, and it just means that once you become a believer, your job is to say no to your sinful self and yes to God and his law in your life. You refuse

Frenemies

to give in to or to please your worldly desires, and you start to think spiritually. You want what God wants instead of what your flesh wants (see Galatians 5:16). When you do that, you're truly a good friend. Imagine a world where no one was looking out only for themselves, but where everyone was looking out for everyone else. It would be . . . well, it would be heaven. According to God's law, you need to use friendship as an opportunity to die to all the ideas that run through your head about what you think you need and to live for the spiritual needs of your friends.

Obviously, dying for a friend or even dying to self isn't about your physical life and doesn't mean there's gotta be blood involved, but what it may require is that you to take good, long, hard look at yourself and find out where you're making life about you. God's Word never talks about pleasing yourself, finding yourself, self-esteem, or self-confidence. He never asks you to get what you want, to be treated the way you want, or to fight for what you want. But what he does do is tell you that your worldly desires are evil and that you need to kill your sinful nature. You have to say no to the things most people fight for. You have to choose to die to yourself and live to serve him (see Romans 6:2–4, 6–7).

What that means practically is that you have to look up. Use Christ as your example. He didn't fight to be treated as the king he was. In fact, he gave up that right when he became a lowly human (see Philippians 2:6–8). And he asks you to do the same thing. In order to imitate Christ, you have to stop being worried about yourself. Look at life from an eternal perspective and put what really matters first: your relationship with Christ. When you do, you'll find yourself less damaged by your frenemy's attacks and more able to give back the love she needs instead of the anger you really wanna hand her.

One of the easiest things to do when someone is offensive is to be offended. You get offended because you are either angry or hurt by what someone says or does. Both reactions are the opposite of holy. Use Christ as your example: "Christ never verbally abused those who verbally abused him. When he suffered, he didn't make any threats but left everything to the one who judges fairly" (1 Peter 2:23). Your reactions to her meanness have to be holy, no matter how bad she makes you feel. You can't make this about your sinful emotions and desires; make it about keeping your eyes on him.

In *Mean Girls*, I wrote about how when you get offended, you just give her the fuel to keep being mean. For a lot of girls, your offended reaction just confirms to them that they're getting through to you. It gives them inspiration. That might not be the case with your frenemy, but it's something to think about. Are you just adding fuel to the fire when you get back in her face or cry or fight with her? Would things be better all around if you just ignored her or walked away? What would happen if you were unaffected by what she said—would it shock her? Give it a try and see what happens when you do it more and more. You might just find that your inability to be rattled has a positive impact on her and on your relationship.

Frenemies

A Friend Draws You Closer to God

A true friend is someone who draws you closer to God and who he wants you to be. This friend is the opposite of the frenemy who draws you away from God. A true friend's goal is never what she wants but always what God wants, and because of that she never leads you anywhere near sin but encourages you to stay spiritually strong. God's Word says, "We should help others do what is right and build them up in the Lord" (Romans 15:2 NLT). A friend is made for encouragement and building up, not discouragement and tearing down. You and your friends should always be drawing each other closer to God, not away from him. So, practically speaking, how do you do that when you have a frenemy who is making your life miserable?

First of all, find ways to have conversations about God. If she's up for following God's way then maybe you could find a good Bible study to do together. I have a few you could try, or you might like others that are out there. Set a date when the two of you can get together and put the focus on God. Don't make it about you and your feelings, but make it about him and his thoughts. And if she's anti-Bible then of course you aren't going to whip out a Bible study, but you can still talk to her about who Jesus is and help her to understand who you are because of that. Make it your role to always draw the relationship closer to him.

If she's asking you to sin with her, remind her of your commitment to God's Word. Have verses to support your beliefs. And don't budge, letting her backslide with your help. Be the stronger sister. Rely on him instead of her to hold you up. Read up—find a book that will help you with whatever problem you see in your life or hers. Get the information you need so that you can be a leader and a helper instead of a victim. Empower yourself with God's Word and counsel from others who love him. Be prepared, in season and out, to give a reason why you believe and to say what you believe (see 1 Peter 3:15). Don't be unprepared so that her choices automatically become yours. Always be prepared to lead her toward God. God will give you the strength to keep the main thing the main thing if you're only willing to make that your number one goal in life.

A Friend Encourages You

A friend is someone who encourages you with God's Word. That means they remind you of verses that will help you in the tough times, or they remind you of who God is when you're feeling lonely and weak. A friend  is an important person in the life of a believer. They're your helper and your protector in times of trouble. They encourage your soul and bring life to your heart. A friend finds so much strength in God's Word herself that she has to share it with you too. "Therefore, encourage each other and strengthen one another as you are doing" (1 Thessalonians 5:11).

As friends, you should be able to count on each other to always bring the subject back to what matters most. That means that if she's struggling with something and maybe even taking it out on you, you can remind her what God's Word says about her particular problem. Do your research and find verses that

Frenemies

you know will meet her where she is and give her some hope. When she hurts you, don't clam up or get nasty back at her. Stop and think about God. What would he want you to say right now? How can you make it about him instead of you? Make it your goal as a friend to speak verses to her throughout the day. Not only will it help her, if she is willing to take help, but it's gonna help you.

A Friend Wants the Best for You

A friend wants only what's best for you. She is going after God and knows his ways, and so her desires for you are in line with his. That means she won't be leading you to sin, at least not intentionally. Her goal is to follow Christ and not the world. That means if something a godly friend says hurts you, you have to consider that it might just hurt because it's reacting with a sin in your life that doesn't want to let go. That's why Scripture tells us that "wounds from a sincere friend are better than many kisses from an enemy" (Proverbs 27:6 NLT). The wound from a true friend is meant to drive you back to God, while kisses from your enemy are meant to separate you from him. You can't always look to how you feel as a guide for how good a friend you have, because a lot of times a good friend will hurt you when she confronts you with your own problems. That doesn't give her free reign to slam you, cut you down, or judge you, but it does give her freedom to speak truth to your dark parts—the parts of you that you try to keep hidden from God.

You should be able to talk with a friend about what's important, but you also have to be willing to be wrong. You can't always know what's best for your friend, but you can always trust God with her life. That means you don't have to overreact to her choices but you can just calmly talk to her about the things she's doing that are hurting you or herself. When it comes to wanting what's best for your friend, you have to make sure that you are never acting out of jealousy or envy, wanting just what you want out of the situation, but are always thinking of what's best for her, like she should be doing for you.

Just because she's missing this part of friendship doesn't mean you join her. What's important isn't what she is or isn't doing but how you are honoring God with your words and your thoughts. If the way she is acting or treating you is wrong, then you, as a friend, are obligated to let her know. If you hurt her, or even if she gets mad, at least you did what you were called to do. Now, this isn't free reign to criticize her every move—you have to pray about things before you dive in and get after her—but it does mean that when you've prayed about it and even gotten advice from someone wiser than you, then you can and should say something if that would be best for her spirit.

A Friend Shares in Your Success and Your Trouble

A friend shares in your success as well as your trouble. She isn't jealous of your wins, because she knows they were a gift of God, and how rude it would be to judge or be disgusted with a gift that God gave! But she's also there for you in times of trouble. She doesn't run off when things get rough. Even when you mess up royally, she's still there. Unless you have walked away from God and are refusing to hear anything from him, she believes in you and sticks

Frenemies

with you, standing by your side until you can get back up on your feet.

Proverbs 17:17 in the New Living Translation goes like this: "A friend is always loyal, and a brother [sister] is born to help in time of need." That means that your friend was born, she was made, to help you out of trouble—not to create trouble but to help you handle any trouble the world sends your way. A friend always has your back, at least as far as God wants her to. In other words, you can't expect a friend to have your back in the area of sin; that wouldn't be a friend but a frenemy.

In order to be a friend who shares in the good times and the bad times, you have to resist the temptation to whine or complain when you don't have something that she has, like a beautiful smile or perfect skin. You can't make her feel guilty for being happy or content just because you don't have what she has. And when she's in trouble or her heart is broken, you have to take the time to let her cry on your shoulder. Be sad that she's sad and happy that she's happy. That's what real friends are for: to share your burdens and your happiness.

Being a friend is a noble pursuit. It calls for faith and love. With faith you believe that God's commands on your life are good for you and for the people around you, and with love you have the power to be just who God wants you to be. Jesus talks about who his friends are in the book of John, and this is how he describes them: "You are my friends if you obey my command-ments" (John 15:14). Being a friend of God—that is, obeying his Word—will make you the best friend another human being can have because God's commandments were made to create in you all the ability to love unselfishly, to believe unceasingly, and to hope eternally. If you want to be a good friend, then learn to be a friend of Jesus.

Spiritual Maturity

Knowing how to be a friend is always the first step in solving the problem of the frenemy. It's important to understand what is expected of both of you in a friendship before you start trying to change things. Now that you've had a quick look at the most important parts of friendship, let's talk about the next step in the process of making things better, and that is thinking about her spiritual maturity. Spiritual maturity will have a huge effect on your relationship with your frenemy and all your other friends as well. So before you write someone off as an unchangeable frenemy, let's take a look at where she sits on the spiritual maturity chart of your life.

I can think of a lot of my friends who on the surface look like frenemies. When we're together it's always about them. I'm forever helping them out of problems and working through trials with them. But to me they aren't frenemies; they're just friends in need. The next question you should ask before you make a change in the relationship is whether your difficult friend is a frenemy or just a friend in need of spiritual growth. So let's do a spiritual maturity inventory, shall we?

I want you to think of five of your closest friends, including one who you think is a frenemy. Write their names down below here, and next to each friend draw an arrow pointing up if you think they are more spiritually mature than you or an arrow pointing down if you think they are less spiritually mature than you. If you think they're just about even with you, then put an equal sign.

Spiritual Maturity Chart

Friend's name: =

_____   _____

_____   _____

_____   _____

_____   _____

Now let's see what all this means. I believe that a Christian should have three kinds of believers as friends. First, you should have a friend who is more spiritually mature than you. This is the friend you go to with your problems, ask what is the biblically right thing to do, ask for prayer, and other spiritual stuff like that. She is a guide for you, a help, a discipler. She might be older than you, and she is definitely wiser than you. Second, you need a friend who is about the same as you when it comes to spiritual stuff. You two understand each other, you pray for each other, and you help each other out, but you're on even ground; one isn't more needy than the other. And finally, I believe we all should have a friend who is less spiritually mature than us. This is the friend who maybe just got saved or who needs a lot of help working on some issues. She isn't as wise as you and needs someone she can go to when life gets confusing. You are her guide to the feet of Jesus.

You are gonna play a different role in the friendship depending on which type of friend you're dealing with. I don't expect my friends who are less spiritually mature than me to listen to me as much as I listen to them. I don't get mad when every time they call it's to ask me for help and not to find out how I am doing. I'm not angry when they get mad at me or say something nasty, because I know my role in the relationship and I am happy to be the more spiritually mature one who can deal with trauma better than they can. With this friend, instead of focusing on my needs, I focus on helping her understand how God's Word relates to her life.

When it comes to your frenemy, the one you are thinking of as you read this book, the first thing you have to think about is her spiritual maturity level. And with that thought in mind, think about her actions and her words. Could some of the things that bother you about her or some of the signs of a frenemy you are seeing in her be a sign of her spiritual immaturity? If you wrote a down arrow beside her name, meaning that she's less spiritually mature, what are some things you can do to change the way you think about her? When you look at friendship in the light of spiritual maturity, handling difficult people becomes a lot easier.

Now, if the friend you think is a frenemy has an equal sign or especially if she has an up arrow by her name, then that gives you something else to think about. At the point when things move from you being more spiritually mature to you two being equal or her being more mature than you, something has got to change. That is to say that if you see some inconsistency between who she is and who she says she is, something is wrong. And knowing that will help you to know how to deal with this frenemy as well.

You have to set higher standards for people who are equally or more spiritually mature than you. But for friends who have it less together spiritually than you do, you have to think of them as weaker in the faith and so you'll need to treat them accordingly. "We who are strong ought to bear with the failings of the weak and not to please ourselves" (Romans 15:1 NIV). If you have a frenemy, you can't fix the problem until you consider the source.

Now, that doesn't mean that if your frenemy is less mature, you put up with all her sin; it just means that you can start to have a better perspective on her actions and start to think of how you should deal with them so you can lead her towards the light and away from the darkness. And if your frenemy has an up arrow, meaning that you think that she is more mature, maybe she's a hypocrite and you shouldn't be looking to her for spiritual guidance. Let's look closer at how to deal with these three kinds of frenemies.

THE LESS SPIRITUALLY MATURE FRENEMY

Let's start with the frenemy with a down arrow. When you realize you are dealing with someone less mature, the first thing you'll need to do is to change your way of thinking. Maybe up 'til now you were thinking of her as your equal—a friend who should give and take equally; a friend you could count on, lean on, and even learn from. After all, that's what a friend is supposed to be to us, right—an equal? But what if she isn't your spiritual equal but is a much weaker sister? You can't expect as much of her. It's not that you shouldn't *want* as much out of her, but right now you have to deal with her where she is.

So let's think about this relationship with a spiritually weaker sister. She needs you. She needs you to be the levelheaded one—the one who doesn't get angry or jealous; the one who isn't offended or fearful. After all, you're the strong one here. You know more about faith, and you have more evidence of faith in your life in the form of the fruit of the Spirit. That means that you shouldn't be easily moved by her or take her shenanigans personally. You have to look at everything through the lens of discipleship. What can you do to help her to know God more? If I demanded that every woman I hang out with be someone I can let it all hang out with and that they all be as spiritually strong as me, then I would have a lot fewer friends than I do. With these kinds of spiritually weaker friends, I can only require that they continue to want to grow and to hear God's truth from me.

Unfortunately, some friends don't want anything at all to do with God's Word. They find it stupid, boring, or even offensive. In these kinds of relationships, it's almost impossible to take a leadership role, because they have no interest at all in following. So your number one job is to love her. It is through that love that she might, just might, come to know Christ. That is a lot on your shoulders, because it means you have to stop making life about you and make it all about him. If she is leading you to sin, you have to stop, period. You are his representative in her life, so you have to show her truth, not fear or disobedience. She might never come to know Christ if her image of you is one of hypocrisy.

The second thing that you have to think about about with this kind of friend is the amount of time you spend with her. One of the reasons she might be making you angry and depressed is because you mistakenly have put more responsibility on her to care for you than she is spiritually capable of. You can't expect the spiritually weaker friend to guide you, to lift you up when you are weak, or to respond to you in the same way someone spiritually equal to you or above you might respond. So, the spiritually weaker friend can't be your best friend. She can't be the one you spend the most time with because that kind of friend needs to be your equal, someone you can count on and lean on in times of trouble. If you spend too much time with the spiritually im- mature friend, she can have more influence on you than you have on her, and that can lead you in a bad direction. With the spiritually weaker friend, it's always best to cut back the amount of time you hang out together to something more manageable, like getting together once or twice a week, tops.

The thing you have to always remember is that you have to be the leader. That means you can't put the weight of your prob- lems on her, because she isn't spiritually strong enough to bear it, and that can lead her astray. Just like a good parent doesn't tell their kids all about the overdue taxes or their troubles at work, the friend who is more spiritually mature doesn't tell her less mature friend all about her traumas and worries. Instead, she thinks about herself as the leader in the relationship and, because of that, stands strong in times of testing and trauma. She knows that as a leader, she can and should rise above and focus on helping, caring for, and training the weaker friend. I'm not asking you to pretend as if you are perfect, just don't lean on her as your source of hope and strength.

When you start to look at the friend who is weaker spiritually from this perspective, you can start to let go of some of your fears, worries, and concerns about the role she should be playing in your life. When your relationship with this friend becomes less about you and your emotional needs and more about her and her spiritual needs, then things will start to come into the light (Ephesians 5:14) and you will start to see more clearly what you should be doing next.

THE EQUALLY SPIRITUALLY MATURE FRENEMY

This is probably what you'll find in most cases of frenemies: you are both equally mature and equally immature. You both have areas in your life that need work, and sometimes those areas just feed on each other. It's normal; friends can bring out the best and the worst in each other. But with the friend who is equally spiritually mature, you have a different standard to live by than you do with the weaker sister. In the previous situation, you were

the leader, the stronger one who was guiding your friend. In this relationship, the guiding is mutual, so you should both be doing your fair share. But for some reason things are off. She seems to be falling into sin more and more, and she is pulling you along with her. This kind of friend should be held to a higher standard. You aren't discipling her; you are sharing your life with her, trusting her, and leaning on her.

When she pulls the rug out from under you or pushes you over, you have two choices. You can either start to consider her the weaker sister and try to help her get back on track. Or, you can decide that she won't

Frenemies

be led anywhere and refuse to let her continue to bring sin into your life either by sharing it with you or by leading you to it as a response to her behavior. Some friends who are used to being your equal, spiritually, might flare up when they start to feel you taking the lead and attempting to direct them back to holiness, but some might appreciate it. You never know until you try.

This kind of frenemy is hard to deal with, but we will continue to dissect how best to approach her and to heal the relationship. Ultimately, what God wants is reconciliation, or restoration of friendship, for his people (see Luke 17:3–4). But when you have tried everything commanded in Scripture, it might just be time to cut ties all together. We'll get into that in a while.

THE MORE SPIRITUALLY MATURE FRENEMY

Wow, this one seems the hardest to bear. She's more spiritually mature than you, but she is dragging you away from God and toward all kinds of fear, worry, and other sin. You have needed her to guide you and to help you to better understand this life of faith, and now all of a sudden it's like things have flipped. If you think that your frenemy is more spiritually mature than you, then there are three possible problems: (1) you were wrong, and she isn't more mature than you; (2) she is more mature, and you are taking the things she says and does the wrong way; or (3) she's backsliding.

Let's look at the first possibility: you were wrong. That might be the case; she might have put on a good show, but over time and testing, her faith hasn't proved the strongest. When a friend starts to turn and starts living a different life than she used to, you have to be aware of what's going on, and you can't take it personally. Her spiritual weakness is just starting to show. But the question has to be, are you strong enough to take on her issues with the power of God's Word, or is it too much for you to handle? If you were wrong about her maturity, then you've got to reconsider her influence in your life, and you need to decide if you are strong enough to step up and be a leader and not a victim, or if it's time to just walk away. You can't let someone pull you in the wrong direction just because you think she's spiritually mature. If she was, then she wouldn't be walking on you—she'd be walking with you.

Okay, now for number two: you are taking things wrong. There's always the possibility that sometimes you might just be overreacting to your friend's words or actions. Having thick skin is important for believers. We can't go around being offended by everything people say about us (see Colossians 3:13). But that can be easier said than done. The thing to do in this kind of situation is to think about what really matters. Is it what she thinks about you or what God thinks of you? If you are sure she's more spiritually mature than you and she's saying things that hurt you, then it's possible that she isn't trying to hurt you, you're just being too sensitive. I'm not saying that's the case—only you can know that—but it's something to think about.

Finally, your friend turned frenemy might just be backsliding into a life of sin. Where she used to be focused on God, she's now focused on herself and the world around her. Her faith is suffering, and because of that, so are you. In this situation, you have an obligation as a fellow believer to bring this condition

Frenemies

to her attention. You can't see a backslidden friend and do nothing. For some reason we as fallen human beings can be blind to our own sin, and so when someone points it out, if we truly want to serve God, we see the light and turn away from our bad ways.

When you have a friend who pretends to be or even believes she is spiritually aware and mature but still acts like people who have no such spiritual awareness, then you have a problem. In this situation, you have a friend who is lying to herself and to you. You have to stop thinking of her as more spiritually mature and start thinking of her as she is: weak and broken. You can't take her rants personally, but look at them from God's perspective. Where is she hurting, where is she needing direction, and where can you help? In some cases, she will be impossible to help; her arrogance will overwhelm any attempt you make to point out her mistakes. In that situation, you might end up having to walk away, but not before you make sure you've done what you were called to do as a believer, and that is to point out how she is disobeying God and to help guide her back to him using his Word.

Well, I hope I've given you something to think about when it comes to friendship and your frenemy. In every relationship problem, it's always best to look at yourself in the mirror before looking at your friend. You can't start to fix the things between you until you fix things within you. When your life comes to an end and you stand before your God, you will be held responsible not for what your friends did but for what you did.

It's important for you as a believer to understand God's Word and how it applies to your life before you start to look at the lives of others.

> But I tell you not to oppose an evil person. If someone slaps you on your right cheek, turn your other cheek to him as well.
>
> Matthew 5:39

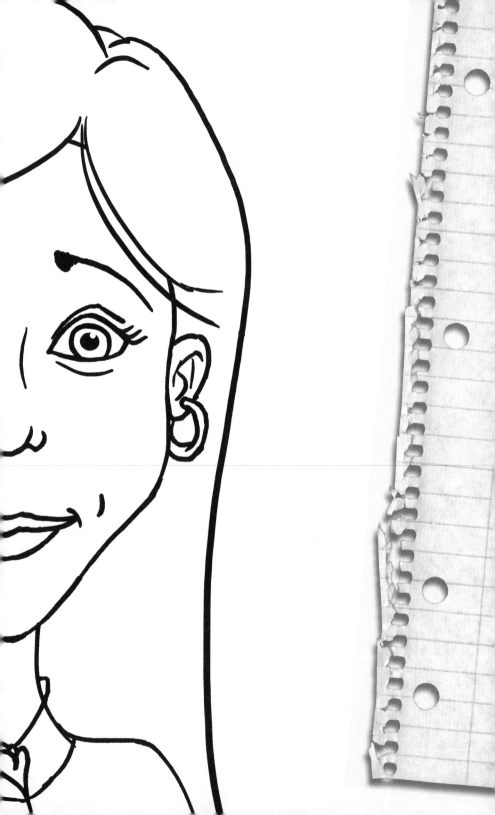

Chapter 3

Fr enemy

Fr̶iend

Taking the Enemy Out of Frenemy

You have a frenemy—you know it for sure. Now what do you
do? How do you help make the relationship better? Regardless
of her level of frenemy-ness, you now have a job to do. Sure,
you could just walk away, block all her calls, and get a new
friend tomorrow, but that's not the most biblical approach. And
you're here to find out what Jesus would do. As a friend of mine
says, God is not a God of chaos. So don't start thinking your life
is now going to be flipped upside down. Before writing off this
frenemy, let's take a look at how you can help take the enemy
out of frenemy.

As far as I'm concerned, we need to look in two places:
inside and outside. That is, what are you believing about God

and his role in your life, and what are you are doing that might be making matters worse?

Looking Inside

I believe that in all relationships, solving problems isn't so much about "them" as it is about "me." That's because there is no power in believing that others need to be changed. In fact, in the Bible, when people were starting to attack each other for their faults, Jesus called them on it and turned the tables back on them when he said, "And why worry about a speck in your friend's eye when you have a log in your own? How can you think of saying to your friend, 'Let me help you get rid of that speck in your eye,' when you can't see past the log in your own eye? Hypocrite! First get rid of the log in your own eye; then you will see well enough to deal with the speck in your friend's eye" (Matthew 7:3–5 NLT). Clearly God knows us better than anyone and understands that none of us are guilt free. None of us should be putting the blame on anyone else until we have taken a long, hard look at ourselves. So that's what I want you to do in this chapter. Be brave, be strong, and be willing to look deep inside to see where you need to be more faithful and holy before you decide where your friend is messing up.

I believe that there are no second causes, but that everything that happens to you is allowed by God into your life for your purification and sanctification—to make you better, stronger, wiser. But the deal with that is that you have to be willing to accept that fact and willing to try to find out what benefit this trial could be to your soul. God promises that he will work all things together for the good of those who love him (see Romans 8:28). If you believe this, then you have to know that this frenemy, this horrible situation, this messy part of your life isn't the end of life as you know it. It isn't even a tragedy, but it's an opportunity for you to be drawn to the God who redeems and makes everything count, including the bad stuff. Your frenemy might be a gift from God to turn you away from the things of this world and back to him. Whatever her purpose in your life, it will never be fulfilled until you are willing to believe that God is in control, that He knows everything you are going through, and that by faith in Him you can not only get through this but also get stronger and healthier because of it.

When you first come face-to-face with a trial, a drama, or a mess in your life, you have to ask yourself, "What does God want me to learn from this?" And your answer shouldn't be "People are messed up and can't be trusted." Does that really sound like something God would say? Obviously not. Finding out what he has to say has to be your priority. And the best place to find it is in his Word. In there, you can learn how he wants you to react to friends, family, and even enemies.

When the tough times come, you gotta open up the Bible. That's one of the beautiful things about hard times: they drive you back to what really matters and force you to need God's Word like you need water to drink and air to breathe. So don't miss this opportunity to plug in to the very God you serve by opening up his words to you and drinking deeply of their goodness and truth. In his Word is the answer to all your heartaches and pains.

Frenemies

In order to take the enemy out of frenemy, you have to realize that God is God and you aren't. Taking your eyes off of your feelings and needs and putting them onto God's desires will start to bring a change to your heart like nothing else. As the Apostle Paul puts it, "All of us will have to give an account of ourselves to God. So let's stop criticizing each other" (Romans 14:12–13). And, let's take a look at ourselves.

The truth of the matter is that you don't have the power to change anyone but yourself, but oh, what power you do have when it comes to you. You think and feel only what you choose to think and feel. "So, brothers and sisters, we have no obligation to live the way our corrupt nature wants us to live. If you live by your corrupt nature, you are going to die. But if you use your spiritual nature to put to death the evil activities of the body, you will live" (Romans 8:12–13). No other human being has the power to control you. But you give up the control that should be yours and only yours when you let her actions control your emotions and when you believe it's your job to fix her. God never calls us to fix others, only ourselves. Sure, you need to encourage, correct, and teach others, but you leave the fixing to God. And you are to focus on yourself when something needs to be fixed. That means that you turn her need to change, her problems, over to him by praying for her and asking him to do what he decides ought to be done.

In life with a frenemy, your freedom comes from a faith in God, not in your friend turned frenemy. I once had a frenemy who was a family member, and that made it hard to get away, hard to hide. They were always there, always picking on me, always pointing out my mistakes, and it was horrible. I would argue, fight, cry, and want to get away, but nothing helped. It just kept on being a trauma almost every day. When I finally stopped obsessing about my frenemy and started to ask God the hard questions, I found not only freedom but also hope and even relief. I started asking questions like, "Why does this person keep saying the same thing? Is there some truth to it? Show me, God, where I need to change. Show me where I'm sinning, purify me, and teach me how to be more like you."

When I got my focus off my frenemy and onto God, things lightened up. I was able to take the negative remarks and turn them into a beautiful tool for my spirit. Whether or not the things said were true, I was still able to not only handle them but also grow and improve in how I communicated with and loved my frenemy. And through that experience I grew in faith and in love, two of the most important things in the life of a believer (see 1 Corinthians 13:13).

FOUR-PART HARMONY

In Webster's dictionary, *harmony* is defined as "internal calm." Imagine having an internal calm that never left you. Wouldn't that be amazing? Wouldn't life be better in that state than in the state of chaos that frenemies can put you in? Well, according to God's Word, harmony isn't just a pipe dream; it's a command. And the good news about commands is that they are all possible to achieve. If they weren't, then they couldn't be commanded.

Frenemies

But wait, there's more. In the New Living Bible, _harmony_ is translated as "being of one mind." So when it comes to relationships, harmony could be described as the relational calm that comes when you agree. But most of the time two people just can't agree on everything. Fortunately, that isn't the end of harmony, because harmony can exist simply when two people agree to some basic principles found in God's Word. Take a look at what God's Word says about harmony and all that goes along with it:

> Finally, everyone must live in harmony, be sympathetic, love each other, have compassion, and be humble.
>
> 1 Peter 3:8

According to this verse, harmony is a command, and so it's a must-have. And the commands that follow harmony all seem to be integral parts of that harmony. You have to live in sympathy, love, compassion, and humility. Everything you need in order to get along with people, even mean people, is summed up right here. But how can you live like that? It sounds good, but what does it really mean? Well, let's take it from the top: sympathy.

SYMPATHY

Merriam-Webster's Collegiate Dictionary says sympathy is "the act or capacity of entering into or sharing the feelings or interests of another." Sympathy is more than just sending a card to someone who lost someone important to them. It's about sharing their feelings and their interests; it's about stepping outside of yourself and into the life of another. And, it's what gives us the ability to understand and to stop our self-obsession. When we get outside ourselves, we get out from under the pressure of internal turmoil and distress. Getting outside of yourself is healthy not only for your heart but also for your relationships.

So how does it look to practice sympathy? I think that first of all it means that when your frenemy does or says something that rubs you the wrong way, your first reaction isn't your self-preservation but an attempt to stand in your friend's shoes and try to understand how she feels and what she wants. It doesn't mean you abandon caring for yourself or your needs, but it does mean that you don't immediately go into self-protection mode and close yourself off to the call on your heart—and that is a call to sympathy, even for someone who is hostile to you.

Obedience to God's Word can't be reserved just for the easy times; in fact, obedience really only proves itself when it's tested. In the hard times, if you can resist the instinct to hide or to fight back and can reach out to the world around you, then you prove that you are who you say you are and that loving God is more important than all the attacks on you and your heart. As a believer, you should react to mean differently than the world does, and that's why Jesus says, "But I tell you this: Love your enemies, and pray for those who persecute you. . . . If you love those who love you, do you deserve a reward? Even the tax collectors do that! Are you doing anything remarkable if you welcome only your friends? Everyone does that!" (Matthew 5:44, 46–47). The remarkable believer is the one who learns to love even when she is being hated. Sympathy draws you out of yourself and teaches you to practice God's command to love even your frenemies. And that brings us to the next ingredient in the recipe for a life of harmony, and that is love.

LOVE

In order to be obedient to God in your relationship with your frenemy, you have to practice love, even when you are getting anything but love in return. Notice that Jesus makes a point of saying that loving those who love you is a piece of cake—anyone can do that, even bad people—but loving people who do not love you but want to hurt you is a special characteristic of the believer (see Matthew 5:44). It's what sets us apart, so when you refuse to act in love, you deny your faith and look like the nonbeliever who can only find the strength to love nice people. Love isn't about what you get in return. It isn't conditional on getting a reward; it is its own reward. And when you can find the strength to put love first, you will find the harmony in your life that your heart craves.

Before we go any further, let's take a little break and do a little frenemy assessment. Take a look at the Qs below and think about you and your frenemy.

I know that love is a big concept, and knowing what love is and isn't can be a major challenge. But God's Word has a lot to say about love, so reading it can help you learn to love God's way. There is so much to loving, but the best description of it is the one you've probably heard a million times. But this time, when you read it, think about each description as it applies to your relationship with your frenemy:

> Love is patient. Love is kind. Love isn't jealous. It doesn't sing its own praises. It isn't arrogant. It isn't rude. It doesn't

think about itself. It isn't irritable. It doesn't keep track of wrongs. It isn't happy when injustice is done, but it is happy with the truth. Love never stops being patient, never stops believing, never stops hoping, never gives up.

1 Corinthians 13:4–7

Have you failed to love your frenemy in any of these areas? Not sure? Then go back for a sec and have a look at your Frenemy Assessment. Look at each question you answered with a yes, and you'll see where you've failed to love like God. But don't freak. We all mess up when it comes to love, but that doesn't mean you can't do or it you should just be happy with what you've got. If you want harmony, then according to God's Word, you've got to learn to love. Love is a decision of your will, and that's good news. It means you can choose right now to start loving.

Try learning the definition of love from 1 Corinthians 13. Memorize it so that you can have it in the front of your mind the next time she does something that tests you. Knowing what is best for you before the problem hits is always the best way to control yourself and your thoughts, and that will bring you a lot more harmony.

COMPASSION

Compassion is the third element of our four-part harmony. According to the dictionary, "compassion implies pity coupled with an urgent desire to aid or to spare." That means you don't just pity someone in trouble, but you also feel a need to help them out of their painful situation. When you have a frenemy, you probably feel like the one who needs the compassion, but

~~~ The Frenemy Assessment ~~~

To find out how well you are dealing with your frenemy, take this quiz:

1. Have you ever lost your patience with your frenemy?
   Yes No
2. Have you ever been mean to your frenemy? Yes No
3. Have you ever been jealous of something your frenemy has or does without you? Yes No
4. Have you ever bragged or tried to get your frenemy to see how amazing you are by giving her a talking-to or arguing with her? Yes No
5. Do you ever feel superior to your frenemy? Yes No
6. Has she gotten on your nerves? Yes No
7. Can you remember every bad thing she's done to you?
   Yes No
8. If so, have you told her some or all of those things?
   Yes No
9. Have you lost hope for your frenemy? Yes No

If you answered yes to one or more of these, then you've got a lot of room for hope. That's because wherever you've answered yes, you've found an area where you can make a change for the better—not by fixing her but by working on you and your relationship with God and his Word. So let's get back into learning about a life of harmony and see where there are some ways change will be possible with you and your frenemy.

as a believer, you can't make it about you; it has to be about those around you who you are commanded to care for. Compassion, like love, isn't something you give only when you get it but is something you give unconditionally.

As hard as it might be, you have to dig deep and find compassion for your friend who is being pulled away from God and his law and toward the sin that entangles her. When you see someone in spiritual pain like your frenemy is, your job is first to try to help guide her back to or toward God with compassion and love. If you've tried all that and she has refused your assistance, it is no longer on you; it's on her for rejecting help.

Humility

Next comes humility. I think that humility is the foundation of all faith. It was in humility that you first went to God and confessed your sin. It is in humility that you continue to trust him as Father God. Humility is the undercurrent of all obedience, and when you refuse to be humble, you risk crashing your faith.

Humility is the best practice in relationships as well. When people start to feel prideful and arrogant, they run the risk of a big fall (see Proverbs 18:12). Pride is not a good component of a good friendship. Humility is what pulls the relationship into the light of God's Word and Spirit.

If humility when it comes to your frenemy is a hard concept for you, then think about how many times you, as a friend and child of God, have acted like God's enemy and so turned into a frenemy yourself. No one is perfect, not even one (see Romans 3:10), and if you are honest, you can see that at times you've messed up too.

As you start to recognize your own weakness and sin, it becomes easier to be humble when you see the same in others.

Entire books have been written on the topic of humility, so I encourage you to do your homework. My favorite is *Humility* by Andrew Murray—you might want to check it out. Read about, study, and talk to people about humility. Figure out how to make it a part of your life. And remember, it was a crucial part of Jesus's life, and if it's a part of Jesus, then why wouldn't you want it to be a part of you as well? "He humbled himself by becoming obedient to the point of death, death on a cross" (Philippians 2:8).

Practically speaking, humility with your frenemy means that you don't always jump to defend yourself, but you first consider where she is coming from. It means that you don't consider yourself better than her. It means that you trust God to fight for you, so you don't think of ways to get revenge. It means that when she's rude, unkind, or downright mean, you aren't hurt or offended by her because you know how unworthy you are of all the blessings God has given you, and what she says only confirms it. When you are truly humble, no one can hurt you with their words, because you base your worth only on the One who saves you and not on another person's opinion of you. Humility is freedom from what people think. Prideful and arrogant people are easily hurt by people's opinions, but humble people can't be shaken. Humility is what makes insults slide off you like water off a duck's back. "God opposes arrogant people, but he is kind to humble people" (James 4:6). Humility leads to success, and pride leads to failure.

A quick note on what humility is not: it's not hating yourself. You can't hate yourself because of who you are, a child of God. Humility is not cutting yourself down or hurting yourself; that would be destroying the temple of God. "Don't you know that your body is a temple that belongs to the Holy Spirit?" (1 Corinthians 6:19). Humility is not destructive; it's life giving and God honoring. If you're thinking something that is inconsistent with Scripture, then you aren't being humble, but disobedient. So beware of confusing humility with self-loathing or insecurity. Humility is the opposite of those feelings, it's the ultimate sign of security in the ultimate power, God. Remember, Christ was truly humble—not weak, not fearful, not inflicting pain on himself but humbled by the power of almighty God. So to learn the practice of humility it pays to study people who understand it and live it. Seek out God's thoughts on the subject, and crave it in your life.

You might find that you and your frenemy can never come into complete harmony, but that shouldn't stop you from working on harmony for yourself by being in step with God's Word. Living in internal calm, or harmony, can start to be achieved when you obey what God's Word says about sympathy, love, compassion, and humility.

EXERCISE

This might seem like a weird suggestion, but get some exercise. When you exercise, your body releases endorphins and you get a natural high. You feel good, your load lightens, and your emotions relax. When you live a life without exercise, your

Frenemies

body weakens, and a weak body doesn't help you to become a strong person. More is going on when you exercise than just muscle building: your hormones are balancing, your mind is clearing, and your heart is strengthening. Exercise can be your chance to clear the air of your mind. It relieves stress and can set you free, if only for a time, from the attacks of your frenemy.

If you haven't exercised in a while, it's time to get going. Go for a long walk or run. Lift weights or play ball. Go skating, swimming, or dancing. Just get out and get your heart rate up. The longer you stay inactive, the longer your body and mind keep holding onto anger and frustration. If you want to let those things go, then exercise. It will open up your heart and empty out all that binds it.

Exercise can also give you something to do and somewhere to go that isn't with your frenemy. So find things to do, groups to join, exercise to get, and you will find yourself less bound up in the sickness of the relationship and more set on the healthy side of life.

Eat Right

Eating might sound like it has nothing to do with living with a frenemy, but what you eat affects how you feel. And how you feel affects how you interact with and treat your frenemy. Food plays a crucial role in your life, so it's important to really understand nutrition and how to get the best food for your body into your body.

For example, eating lots of sugary stuff might make you feel good while you are eating it, it might be your escape from your messed-up life, but after you eat it, things aren't so great. As your blood sugar rises and falls, your emotions rise and fall with it. Sugar can make you cranky, weak, hyper, and depressed. If you want to get control of your life, you have to get control of your diet. Do your research; find out what's good for you and what isn't. Do some foods give your body energy? Do some give you strength? Find out. I can remember drinking fresh orange juice whenever I was stressed. Fresh-squeezed orange juice actually releases endorphins in your body, like the kind that runners get when they run, that make you feel good. Sugar can do that for a while, but coming down from sugar can send you into a disastrous spiral. When you feed your body healthy food, your emotions start to level out, and that gives you not only happiness but also self-control.

You can't let your emotions be your guide when it comes to eating. Learn what is healthy and eat that. It might be hard at first, but the more you do it, the better you will feel. Eating right is your weapon against fatigue, depression, and anger. Your body needs proper nourishment in order to perform at its best. So refusing to eat, eating and purging, or eating too much only weakens your self-control and your ability to find peace and hope in your situation.

If you have a problem with food, then this is your chance to do something about it. In fact, this is your *call* to do something about it. The thing to think about is that when God wants to get your attention, to reveal something to you, and you don't listen or pay attention, he keeps on letting things in your life happen that will get you to see where the work needs to be done. It's like taking a test that you're gonna be given over and over again until you finally pass. Could your family frenemy be the attention-getter God sent for your body and how you treat it? You'll never know and you'll never stop the testing until you pass the test. So don't let this opportunity to improve yourself go to waste. When you take advantage of the test and work to pass it, you just might find that the testing stops.

Looking Outside

Now that we've had a look from the inside out, let's have a look at the outside: your actions. When it comes to your role in relationship with your frenemy, you can't always blame it all on her. A lot of the time friends grow into frenemies because they're allowed to do so. In *Mean Girls*, I talk about how some girls are easy targets for mean. If you have a Mean Girl in your life, it might be because you've made yourself a target that she can easily hit. The same can be true of your frenemy. You may just have made yourself an easy target for her meanness. But don't worry—you can do something about your status as a target. It can take time to change, but it can be changed, and you *can* get the red circles off your back.

Is It You?

The first thing I think we need to look at is you and your actions, and not just how you act with your frenemy. Maybe, just maybe, you are doing something that is fueling her mean. We all have little things we do that bother or frustrate other people.

Think about the things the people you live with do. What little things make you crazy whenever they do them? That kind of stuff can be difficult for friends to handle too. So before you put all the blame on your frenemy, let's check out how you look on the outside. Start by answering these questions honestly:

1. What do you do at home that irritates the people you live with?

2. Do you do anything that more than one of your friends says bothers them about you? In other words, is there a problem you've heard about more than once?

3. Have you ever criticized your friend for doing something you do yourself?

4. What would you like to change about yourself that might make your relationships easier (for example, an anger problem or shyness)?

5. Make a list of people in your life who you have had a hard time getting along with.

Now, looking back over the relationship problems you have, and see if there's anything that seems to repeat itself. Repeated situations can give you a good hint into that something you are doing might be wrong. It's like this: if a woman tells me that she has been divorced three times and she just can't find a good

Frenemies

man, I'm going to take a long shot and say that maybe the *men* aren't the problem. After all, who is the common denominator in these bad relationships? She is.

It's time to do some real self-assessment to make sure that you aren't giving your frenemy the urge to be mean. If you think anything you're doing might be encouraging her attitude, then maybe it's time to ask for her forgiveness and to make some changes. In fact, if you've been a pain to the people in your life, then it might be time to make the rounds. Come clean and apologize for how you've behaved.

People Pleaser

Is acceptance important to you? If it's super important, then you might have a problem with your need to please. When you have an overly powerful desire to get her acceptance, you give her the power to control you. And for a lot of girls, that's just too hard to resist. Their sinful nature just kicks in, and they overtake you with mean.

As a believer, you can't let yourself be controlled by anyone but God. When you do, you sin. So consider the fact that if you're a people-pleaser and you let yourself be controlled then it's not just her fault but yours as well.

What's at the root of your inability to say no to her? Fear? Insecurity? Or do you just think that you have to let her be in charge in order to keep her as your friend? If any of these reasons sound right to you, then it's time for a change. No healthy person wants a friend who is afraid of her, and your insecurity is only encouraging her sin. If you can look at things from a more spiritual perspective, you can get free from this position you've put yourself in.

The way you break free is by realizing that you have put your frenemy on the throne where God used to be. Jesus says to walk a mile with your enemy (see Matthew 5:41), but that doesn't mean obeying her to get something you want, like her friendship. And that's the thing, the root of her control is your need to get something from her. You might just want peace, but the cost of that peace shouldn't be your obedience to her. So think about why you do what she asks, and then ask yourself if your reason is sinful. Then you have to make a choice: do I choose to defy her or God?

THE EASY TARGET

Another thing to think about fueling the fire of the frenemy is how you react to her nasties. A lot of times when you react the wrong way to her attacks or slams, you just make things worse. Arguments happen, things get out of hand, and trouble hits. The best thing to do is to stop, take a deep breath, and think about what's really going on. In the life of your friend, you're supposed to be a reminder of God, not a chance for a fight. If you never let her push you into sin, she'll more than likely change her ways. Or you'll at least give her a chance to see how smart girls handle conflict. When you react in anger, crying or screaming, you give her a degree of power that she shouldn't have and can't handle. So hold on to your emotions, don't get all dramatic over the situation, and you'll maintain the control you need. If she's just too much to handle, then get away 'til she cools off. Don't make yourself an easy target, and don't fuel the fire of mean.

EASY TO CONTROL

Most friends of frenemies need to learn not to let her control them. The only control you should be under is the control of the Holy Spirit. If you let her be your dictator and tell you how to think, act, or speak, then you've betrayed God. It might be hard to refuse a frenemy, but you have the strength in you by the grace of the Holy Spirit. That means that you have the power to say no to anything that she wants you to do or feel that is unbiblical. Know the Word. Study God's law so that it will always be your first response to testing and so that you will never let anyone or anything else control you.

You can't always blame everything on your frenemy. Some of the ways that you are acting around her might be making things worse. If you can find some things, don't freak out; just be glad that you now know some things you can change. And maybe those little changes will make a difference in your relationship.

Confronting Your Frenemy

Friends are meant to build each other up and to point one another toward God, you've probably gotten that by now. And that can sometimes mean you've got to confront and even be confronted on the blind spots in your life. And, who better than a friend who knows you well to help you see your weakness? Confronting your friend can be really hard, even painful, but you have a responsibility to gently guide her back on track, or at least to start the process (see Colossians 3:16; 2 Timothy 3:16).

I hope you agree that not only is your friend a sinful human being, but so are you. Knowing that, you can humbly say that you both might have things you need to work on. So when it comes to confronting, you might try the "you help me and I'll help you" approach. Humility is always better received than arrogance. And when a friend is being confronted on her meanness, she might feel like you are being holier-than-thou unless you add yourself to the mixture.

In other words, you can try saying something like this: "I'm having some problems with sin in my life, and I need to talk to you about it." Then talk about the sin that she encourages in you. Tell her that you need her help because for some reason when she does this or that, you tend to fall into sin. Tell her you don't want to blame everything on her, you just want to be a true friend and work together to get the sin out of your relationship. When you can make it about you as much as her, she will be less likely to get as defensive.

Of course, it might be a case where it's all her and not you. In that situation, you might need to just get to the point and help her to see where she's walking away from God and his law. A lot of times, people can get off track just by force of habit. You do something enough times and suddenly it becomes a regular thing. You can't assume that your frenemy even knows of all her idiosyncrasies and sins, but you also can't plan to be the one who fixes her. When it's time to have "the talk," you have to think about a lot of things, and I'll go over a lot of what you'll need in the next chapter, so don't skip over that one. But for now, what you need to know is some of God's thoughts on helping your friends:

> If people are causing divisions among you, give a first and second warning. After that, have nothing more to do with them. For people like that have turned away from the truth, and their own sins condemn them.
>
> Titus 3:10–11 NLT

In that verse, what is the problem with the "people"? Does that sound like your frenemy?

What do you think "give a first and second warning" means?

What is the third thing you do if the first two don't make things different?

Why do you think Paul is so harsh with these people?

> Brothers and sisters, if a person gets trapped by wrongdoing, those of you who are spiritual should help that person turn away from doing wrong. Do it in a gentle way. At the same time watch yourself so that you also are not tempted.
>
> Galatians 6:1

What is another word for wrongdoing?

Is your frenemy trapped by wrongdoing?

What are you asked to do for her?

How are you called to do it?

What else do you have to watch when you're with her?

Part of confronting is knowing yourself and your God. If you aren't solid in your faith and you don't know that you can stand up to her arguments, then you might not be ready to talk with her. Take time to find out what God's Word says about her particular sin of choice. Talk to your pastor or mentor to get some advice on how best to talk to her about her sin. If after a lot of study, prayer, and counsel you decide she isn't sinning, but just being insensitive or oblivious to what she's said or done, then you can still talk with her, but be sure that you focus on how her behavior makes you feel. Always speak humbly and trust that when you do, she is less likely to freak out than if you are being aggressive.

Remember, your goal shouldn't be getting even or getting her to agree with you, but your goal should be getting her to hear God's Word so that she can decide for herself what she will do. You don't have to win this one; you just have to get God's Word into her head.

But before you do any of this, you need to think about what kind of frenemy she is. I'll talk about three different types in the next chapter, so get ready to find out more that will help you win the battle to take the enemy out of your frenemy.

Fr enemy

Fr iend

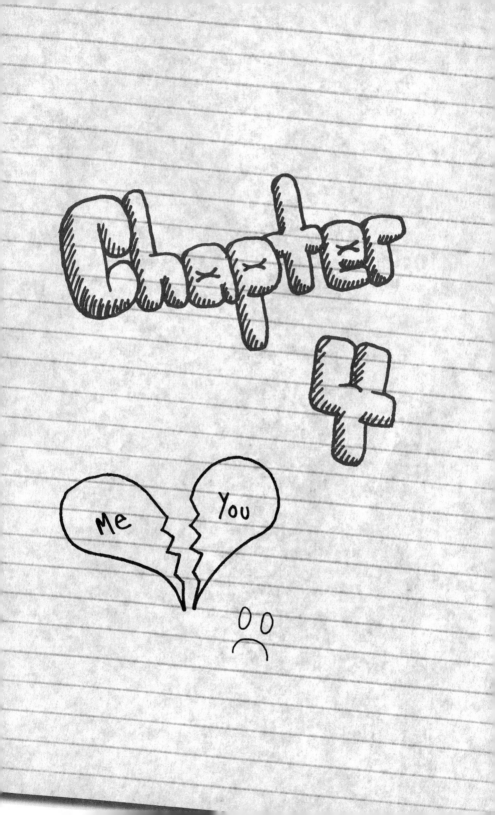

How to Break Up with Your Frenemy

How's it going? Have you taken the enemy out of frenemy? Have you taken a good, long, hard look at yourself and made the necessary spiritual adjustments? Dealing with a frenemy is a complicated thing; you have a lot of options and a lot of things to consider. But how do you know when you've given it your all and it's time to walk away?

The friend part of the equation can make breaking up hard to do. You love her, or at least you did. You want her back. You wish things could be like they used to. You like her when she's nice but hate when she's mean. You've seen how she can hurt you, and now you know how she can lead you away from God, and you don't want all the drama and pain anymore. So is this friendship over? It's hard to know for sure; only you can really say. But if you've given this situation a lot of thought, prayer, and attention, then it might be time to make some changes.

I believe that our God is a God of reconciliation. Jesus said, "So if you are offering your gift at the altar and remember there that another believer has something against you, leave your gift at the altar. First go away and make peace with that person. Then come back and offer your gift" (Matthew 5:23–24). He doesn't want us to fight, hate, or abuse. He wants us to forgive, heal, and accept. From looking at that verse, you can tell that he wants us to have a sense of urgency about reconciliation in our lives. And so I have no doubt that our first response to conflict should always be working through it instead of running away from it. But there comes a point when enough is enough—when you've tried all you can to heal the bad parts of the relationship and nothing has worked, and she's still distracting you from your God. Are you at that point? Have you come to the end of the road?

Giving up on people who refuse to see that light isn't an unbiblical approach. After giving it some effort and prayer, sometimes the right thing to do is to just walk away. The apostle Paul had to do that with a couple of his friends. He wrote about it and said, "Some have refused to let their faith guide their conscience and their faith has been destroyed like a wrecked ship. Among these people are Hymenaeus and Alexander, whom I have handed over to Satan in order to teach them not to dishonor God" (1 Timothy 1:19–20). I'm not saying it's your job to hand your friend over to Satan. What I am saying is that sometimes enough is enough and the ship is wrecked beyond what your small hands can repair. And that's when it's time to break up.

If you've tried everything you've read so far in this book and you're still being sucked in by your frenemy's sin, then it might just be time to end it all with her. You can't let yourself get off track spiritually because of your loyalty to her. God's Word gives you an out in this situation:

> Your own brother, son, or daughter, the wife you love, or your best friend may secretly tempt you, saying, "Let's go worship other gods." (Those gods may be gods that you and your ancestors never knew. They may be the gods of the people around you, who live near or far, from one end of the land to the other.) Don't be influenced by any of these people or listen to them. Have no pity on them. Don't feel sorry for them or protect them.
>
> Deuteronomy 13:6–8

You can't feel sorry for her or protect your friendship if it's time to stop the sin cycle. You can't put her feelings and friendship over your friendship with God. If you've been led away by  her into obeying anyone other than him and you feel powerless to change that, then it's time to think about a break up. James says,

> But don't just listen to God's word. You must do what it says. Otherwise, you are only fooling yourselves. For if you listen to the word and don't obey, it is like glancing at your face in a mirror. You see yourself, walk away, and forget what you look like. But if you look carefully into the perfect law that sets you free, and if you do what it says and don't forget what you heard, then God will bless you for doing it.
>
> James 1:22–25 NLT

In these pages, you've read God's Word and you've heard my thoughts, and now you have to make a decision. Will you take

Frenemies

what you now know and act upon it, or will you fall back into your destructive habits of following her lead? She was never meant to lead you. It's up to you as the stronger believer, the one who sees the sin and wants to end it, to lead her. And leading her might mean that you lead her in the opposite direction of you. Sometimes walking away is the best thing you can do for her. It might just get the point across to her better than anything else you could say or do.

But with all that said, breaking up can't be taken lightly, so let's look at the subtle nuances of breaking up with your frenemy.

Standing Up to Sin

One of the most important steps in changing your relationship with your frenemy is being brave enough to stand up to the sin she brings into your life. You can't continue to obey her *and* be faithful to God. You have to be unafraid to do or say what needs to be done or said in order to make sure that others don't become so dominant in your life that God takes a backseat. Some people call this having healthy boundaries. This is super important with a frenemy because more than likely, they have no boundaries when it comes to you. So before you move into break-up mode, let's look at some ways that you can stand up to her and start to change the dynamic.

She will continue to be your frenemy for as long as you let her, so you have to take back control. No one should control you, and you should never feel guilty for refusing to let them control you. It's natural to feel guilt when you change the way you interact with your frenemy, but you can't let that stop you. Feel what you will feel, but tell yourself that this has to stop and you are strong enough to stop it.

To get you started, let's look at a few ways you can start to stand up to her and her frenemy ways.

5 WAYS TO STAND UP TO HER INVITATIONS TO SIN

First off, let me just say that confronting your frenemy can sometimes make matters worse. So here are some ideas for how you can stop letting her meanness affect you without confronting her personally.

1. **Say no to her invitations.** When she calls to say, "Let's go to the mall," tell her you have things you need to do at home; homework, chores, helping your mom, etc. You don't have to say no every time, but say no often enough, and over time she'll probably stop asking.

2. **Refuse to participate.** When she starts to gossip about someone or slam someone, don't join in. Say you have something you have to do, and walk away. Don't join in on the sin fest.

3. **Don't return all her calls.** When she texts you or calls you, don't call her or text her right back. Nothing says you have to answer right away, or even at all. Answer every third time she contacts you, and then gradually make it less often. If you want to, turn off your ringer and blame it on that. Or ask your parents to keep your phone for

Frenemies

a while so you don't have to deal. Just don't be so quick to call or text her back; nothing says you have to do that. Just put the phone away and walk away; it won't be as hard as it sounds.

4. **Keep conversations short.** When you do talk to her on the phone, keep it short. Plan something that you have to do in five minutes so you won't talk any longer. Let her know you've gotta go because of _____. Then get off the phone no matter how much she protests.

5. **Don't obey her.** If she is used to asking you to do things like getting her a drink or doing her homework, you have to start saying no. Scared to say no? Then come up with a reason why you can't do that thing. You're busy, you're meeting someone, your parents won't let you— whatever. Standing up and refusing to let her control you is always hard and risky. She's going to hate it, but you have to choose between serving her and serving God. And know that her wrath cannot truly hurt you unless you let it.

What Kind of Frenemy Do You Have?

The way I see it, there are three kinds of frenemies: the 1 in 10 frenemy, the 50–50 frenemy, and the 24–7 frenemy. Each one will takes a slightly different tactic in the art of breaking up. So before you do anything, think about her mean. When is she mean? How often is she mean? That's going to make a big difference in how you get the mean out of your life. Take this quiz to get your answer:

Quiz: What Kind of Frenemy Is She?

On a scale of 1 to 10, how often is your frenemy mean in the following situations? Circle 1 if it's hardly ever and 10 if it's all the time.

1. When you are with a group of girls.
   1 2 3 4 5 6 7 8 9 10
2. When she's at your house and your parents have just left after giving you a list of chores.
   1 2 3 4 5 6 7 8 9 10
3. When you are at the mall. 1 2 3 4 5 6 7 8 9 10
4. When you talk to her on the phone.
   1 2 3 4 5 6 7 8 9 10
5. When she's had a bad day. 1 2 3 4 5 6 7 8 9 10
6. When your outfit just isn't working.
   1 2 3 4 5 6 7 8 9 10
7. When you are with a group of guys.
   1 2 3 4 5 6 7 8 9 10
8. When you are depressed. 1 2 3 4 5 6 7 8 9 10
9. When you go to her house. 1 2 3 4 5 6 7 8 9 10
10. When you are in a group of three or more.
    1 2 3 4 5 6 7 8 9 10
11. When you do something she doesn't like.
    1 2 3 4 5 6 7 8 9 10
12. When you talk about God stuff.
    1 2 3 4 5 6 7 8 9 10
13. When you need her. 1 2 3 4 5 6 7 8 9 10
14. When you do better than her at something.
    1 2 3 4 5 6 7 8 9 10
15. When you get something that she wants.
    1 2 3 4 5 6 7 8 9 10
16. When you are with a boy. 1 2 3 4 5 6 7 8 9 10
17. When she disagrees with you. 1 2 3 4 5 6 7 8 9 10
18. When it's that time of the month.
    1 2 3 4 5 6 7 8 9 10
19. When she's tired. 1 2 3 4 5 6 7 8 9 10
20. Whenever she's with you. 1 2 3 4 5 6 7 8 9 10

Frenemies

Now add up your score. _____

Scoring:

20–80: The 1 in 10 frenemy—Your friend isn't mean all the time, just every so often. Maybe she doesn't even realize what she's doing, or maybe she's just got a really weak spot in her personality that leads her to have mean reactions in certain situations. The 1 in 10 frenemy isn't making you crazy; she's just making you wonder what's going on and when she's gonna change. She probably wasn't always mean, or maybe you've just started to notice her mean, but the important thing to remember is how many times you say or do something hurtful yourself. We all can mess up, and we can all be mean. So take heart. The 1 in 10 frenemy isn't the worst frenemy you could have, and you might even be able to fix things so you can avoid almost all of her mean.

81–120: The 50–50 frenemy—So would you say that half the time she's nice and half the time she's a real pain? The 50–50 friend is very unpredictable; you never know when she's going to attack. Just when you think things are going great, she freaks out on you or says something totally hurtful. You have to be on guard all the time with the 50–50 frenemy because you just never know when it's coming. This frenemy has a lot of issues, and getting the mean to stop might take a bit of work on your part. That doesn't mean it can't be done, but it does mean you might end up walking away if she keeps it up.

121–200: The 24–7 frenemy—This is a true Mean Girl. You know exactly what you're going to get from her every day: mean. She left the friend category a long time ago and has moved comfortably into being your enemy. What's going on? When did it all change? And what do you do now? Things have got to stop. You've got to make some changes, but be careful how you do it or you'll have one angry Mean Girl. The 24–7 frenemy has to be treated with kid gloves in order to get the insanity to end. So read carefully and find out how best to get her out of your life. It's not as obvious as it might seem.

Breaking Up 101

Okay, you've taken the quiz, and you may or may not be thinking, *That's totally it.* But whether the quiz nailed it or seemed a bit off, I bet you are starting to get a picture of what kind of frenemy you have. Deep down you know how bad things really are. And how bad things are will have a big effect on what you do next.

Before we get to the art of breaking up with your frenemy, I hope you've covered all the other bases. All the things I wrote about in the last chapter need to be really thought about before

you go to this more nuclear option. In this option, you are going to end the relationship. Things aren't changing—you are, but she isn't. You feel in danger, or you just can't handle it anymore; whatever the reason, you've decided that it would be better for you to take the friend out of frenemy. And that's okay. You don't have to be bff with everyone. You can and should pick and choose who you spend your precious time with. But don't walk away without first making a plan.

The breakup can be done different ways depending on which kind of frenemy you have. Each way is meant to be used with a different kind of girl, and if you do it right, you'll save yourself some heartache. Sure, this relationship will bring some heartache, but at least you can work to make it as painless as possible. When you are dealing with a Mean Girl—and that's what you've got here—you have to be very deliberate and unemotional in your actions. You can't do something that will make things worse.

Frenemies

A complete, never-talk-to-her-again breakup might not be what this relationship needs. Cold turkey doesn't always work in all situations. And in some, just a little more distance will do the trick. What's most important is that you break up the opportunities for her to be mean. For some frenemies, confrontation and correction will work, but for others, that's the worst thing you could do. Standing up for yourself isn't always the best policy. Sometimes the silent breakup is the best thing. It depends who she is and how she's mean. You're going to need to make your exit plan applicable to her personality and proximity. If your frenemy lives at home with you or is a part of your extended family, you might not be able to do any kind of breaking up at all, and I'll cover that situation in the next chapter. But either way, let's take a look at some ways you can start to put some distance between you and your frenemy, starting with how to deal with the 1 in 10 frenemy.

The 1 in 10 Frenemy

If your frenemy is more friend than enemy, her mean might not be something she's even aware of. It might be tied to something going on in her life. Maybe her attacks are hormonal, coming at you once a month, or maybe she has a problem with anger or bitterness, something in her spirit that she wants to control but just has lost control of. The 1 in 10 frenemy probably isn't a frenemy that needs a big breakup. More than likely she's not trying to be mean. She's just having a rough time of things and has lost perspective.

Depending on where she stands in her relationship with God, different things might need to be done. If you've read this book up to this point and applied the ideas of spiritual maturity, sympathy, love, compassion, and humility, and she's still not willing to give up on the mean, then you have a decision to make. Will you keep on practicing godliness around her and just look at her like a "thorn in your flesh" ala 2 Corinthians 12:7–10? Or is it time for a change?

If you choose the first option, then you should know what to do: just keep practicing the things I talked about in the last two chapters. But if you think it's time for a bigger change, then the first thing you need to do is pray about your friend. If you haven't done it already, you've got to get God in the picture, and the way you do that is by praying. Ask God what your role in her life is. Tell him you want to move on, and ask him how to best do that. Nothing says that to love another person you have to be their best friend or even their constant friend. Sometimes you can love people better from a distance, so don't feel bad about wanting to get away from her, but don't be too quick to move on. Spend the next week in prayer about it. Pray and read. Look into God's Word for answers before you do anything drastic.

CONFRONTING THE 1 IN 10 FRENEMY

You knew the day would come, and it finally has. Now it's time for "the talk." If your friend is a 1 in 10, then chances are she's not a Mean Girl, just a weak girl. That means she just might welcome some insight on her mood swings. But when you confront someone on their mean, you need to be clear. So I suggest doing some prep work.

After working through some of the quizzes in this book, you should have a better idea of when and how she's mean. So write down your specific complaints on a piece of paper. List the categories of things that hurt you, like "It hurts me when you make fun of me, yell at me, lie to me, etc. . . ." You shouldn't have a huge list to give her in the end, but just name one or two specific things she's done from those categories to give her an idea of what you are feeling. You don't want to overwhelm her, so try to be specific about the kinds of things and then to have a few examples to give her if she asks for them. I might go something like this, "I feel really bad whenever you make fun of me, like when you pick on my messy room. I feel bad." Don't bring out this list when you are with other friends. Do it one-on-one. That way, she won't be embarrassed. With this frenemy you don't have to come out swinging. In other words, she probably isn't going to argue with you or deny your pain, so you don't have to give her a big list of verses that confirm she's a sinner. That would be overkill. Just share your feelings with her and tell her how important she is to you and how you want to make things better if she is willing.

If she is, then you two could talk more about how you feel and about ways that you could both make some changes in order to fix things. This could be a good time to suggest doing a Bible study together just to keep the dialogue going.

But if she isn't having any of it and argues with you instead of listening to you, and if she refuses to change, but blames you instead, then you've got some more work to do. I always think it's good to soul search on these things to make sure *you* aren't the problem, but if you are sure that her meanness is the cause of your heartache and you don't want to experience it anymore, breaking up might be the best thing to do about it.

BREAKING UP WITH THE 1 IN 10 FRENEMY

You've said your peace. She knows your pain. And now it's time to move on. You can do the quick breakup or the slow breakup. Either method will work; you just have to decide how you want to do it. The quick one has you telling her that you don't feel comfortable hanging out with her because it just encourages you to sin too much. After that, you start making new friends and not to hanging out with each other anymore.

If that sounds too harsh, then you can give the slow method a shot. In this breakup, you just cut back on the things you do together. You figure out what's best for you—group activities, chatting online, or talking on the phone—and you narrow your relationship down to that. Slowly, over time, things will fizzle out. You will each get busy and find new friends, and life will go on.

The 50-50 Frenemy

The 50–50 frenemy comes in a lot of different kinds. Some are completely unpredictable. These friends get mean so randomly that you just never know what's coming next. They can be the hardest to be around because you can't predict what's coming next. You never know if you're gonna get a hug or a trip from her. Other 50–50 frenemies have a more predictable pattern, like they are nice when you are alone but get mean when they are in a group of girls. Or maybe they are your best friend when you are chatting on-line, but when you are face-to-face, they turn into Mrs. Hyde of Dr. Jekyll and <u>Mrs. Hyde</u> fame.

CONFRONTING THE 50-50 FRENEMY

When it comes to confronting this frenemy, you might first need to think about what makes her the maddest. When is she grumpy, nasty, or downright mean? Does it correspond to any type of trigger? That trigger could help you to better diagnose the problem and find the solution.

Breaking up with a frenemy isn't the same as breaking up with a boyfriend. Both can be really hard, but with the frenemy you have the added problem of her mean tendencies. The 50–50 frenemy has Mean Girl tendencies, and when confronted she could act more like a Mean Girl than a friend. And that means you've got to be prepared before you do any confronting.

Have you ever noticed that she is mean in certain situations and not in others? If you aren't completely sure or have never thought about it, answer these questions and see what you can find.

So did you learn anything? Find out something new about her and your relationship? If you can spot certain things or places that make her mean, then maybe you've found a way to avoid the enemy part of this frenemy and keep the friend. It's like this: if she is nasty to you when she's with other girls, then you might have to stop hanging out with her and her other friends.

The Mean Times Questionnaire

Find out when she's the most mean so you know what situations you can change or avoid all together.

1. Is she more mean when you're alone or when you're in a group of girls?
2. Do you feel worse after being with her or after chatting with her online?
3. Is there something she gets especially mad about, like your style, your room, your car, or your family?
4. Think about the last few times she blew up. What was her problem each time?
5. Does someplace you go seem to bring out her nasty side (i.e., the mall, games, parties, her house)?
6. Does her mean repeat in a cycle? In other words, does she get worse when she has PMS or when she just came back from her every-other-weekend with her dad?
7. When was the last time you can remember her being all friend and no enemy?
8. Is she mean to other people too? Who?
9. Does she ever gang up on you?
10. Has she ever said, "I'm sorry"?

Frenemies

It sounds harsh, but you aren't likely to get her to stop seeing them, especially if she's been friends with them for a long time. If she's just started hanging out with these girls and it's affecting your friendship, you can feel free to talk with her about the problem, but usually the best way to deal with that problem is to remove yourself from those situations. You can't change her, but you can change yourself. If you notice that she gets catty and mean whenever you are at the mall, then stop saying yes to shopping trips. A little bit of common sense and a whole lot of humility will help you make these kinds of choices.

If you are certain that this won't be enough and you're ready to say something to your 50–50 frenemy, I would suggest that you spend some time working on an outline of what you are going to talk about. Be prepared for her to get upset.

Before you confront this frenemy, it's best to decide what you're going to say so that things don't get out of control all over again. Having a prepared speech, so to speak, will help you do that. Not that you are going to memorize your lines or anything, but write down the important points that you know you have to say, and an idea of when you'll have covered all you need to covered and how you'll say goodbye.

Go over your notes from this book and make a list of what she does and when she does it. Be specific about the ways she hurts you, making fun, lying, rejecting you, etc. Then write down a few specific instances where she did some of those things. Decide what you want the outcome of the confrontation to be: an intervention or a final goodbye. And if it's a goodbye, then decide how you will say goodbye and when you will walk away.

Figure out the best location to do this discreetly and not in front of a bunch of people, and be sure to go over a few verses that will remind you that this isn't really about her, but about obeying God and refusing to give into the enemy. (Ephesians 6:12)

Then I suggest you go over your ideas a few times, maybe even with your mom or dad. Get it into your head what you're going to say, like "I'm having a trouble with sin in my life. I'm depressed, worried, etc. and I need to spend some more time going after God on these issues. I find that I most often sin in response to some of the things you do or say and because of that I feel like I need to take a break from this relationship." Something like that. Work out some nice ways of saying what you've got to say, but know that no matter how nice you are she's still going to be shocked and probably even a little mean. Big surprise.

BREAKING UP WITH THE 50-50 FRENEMY

When confronted, the 50–50 frenemy will quite possibly blame you for everything and maybe even do the breaking up for you. But if she doesn't run off screaming and you don't want to keep on giving her chance after chance to change, then it's time for you to walk away from the relationship.

If you've been friends for a long time, you're going to have to be prepared for a lot of questions about why you are dumping her friendship. You have to be clear when this happens. You can't fight or start blaming her; you have to just stick to your outline. In other words, talk to her about yourself—how you don't want to sin any longer and how you feel that her actions lead you in the direction of sin. You can have some verses ready, if she is a believer. And be prepared for potentially a long talk. The longer you've been friends, the longer the talk. (Note: if you are new friends, then you really don't even need to have a talk. Casual friends will just disappear without attention.)

Be sure not to break up when her other friends are there. If you are afraid of her, you might need to do it in a public place or at home with your family. But never break up with anyone in front of their friends; it's too humiliating and offers too much opportunity for them to form battle lines and get the help of others around to fight you.

Decide ahead of time what, if anything, will keep you from walking away completely. If she seems truly sorry, then maybe you're ready to work on the relationship. But if she is just bullying you to keep you around, then you have to decide to be firm and to stick to your guns. Remember, though, that if she refuses to hear you or to admit the friendship is over, it's not the end of the world. You don't have to answer the phone every time she calls or be available when she asks you to do things. Part of breaking up is sometimes just saying no to her invitation more often than you say yes, until finally she stops asking.

If the 50–50 frenemy is super angry and unreasonable, then you can just stop the conversation, leave, and decide to not spend any more time with her. In other words, you don't have to convince her of anything if she is unwilling to be convinced.

With the 50/50 frenemy, you might need to be prepared for retribution. She might plan all kinds of ways to get you back and to make sure everyone knows how bad you are. If you're pretty sure that's how she will react, you might want to avoid the breakup altogether and just go right to saying no more often than you say yes. That doesn't mean you can't confront her on her stuff, but maybe you should confront her on one thing instead of all the things. You know her and how she is probably going to react, so be wise. Get wise counsel and know that no law says you have to be friends with her or that you are sinning by breaking up the relationship. You have the right and even the obligation to walk away from people who draw you away from God.

The 24-7 Frenemy

The 24–7 frenemy has got to be the worst. Essentially, she's pure Mean Girl and you've been lying to yourself that she's a friend. You know what you're gonna get from her almost all the time—a hard time. She was nice, once upon a time, but now she seems to be out to get you. You put up with her slams and assaults on your style, your thoughts, and your family, but how much more can you take? The 24–7 frenemy is almost all enemy, and because of that you've got to be strategic in how you break up. You might find yourself on her hit list if you confront her and then let her know that you will no longer be hanging out with her. This girl isn't thinking right. She's put anger and resentment above obedience and love. She will most likely best be helped by prayer right away and not by intervention in the short term.

CONFRONTING THE 24-7 FRENEMY

Mean Girls are a particular kind of beast. They have their own set of rules when it comes to relationships. I wrote *Mean Girls* because I hoped to help girls better understand the mind of the Mean Girl and figure out how best to handle her depending on her style and mind-set. If your frenemy is 24/7 then maybe you could get some more help from *Mean Girls,* so you might want to check it out. You might not have thought of the fact that she's truly a Mean Girl, but maybe it's time to consider that. When it comes to a Mean Girl, you definitely don't want her as an influence, and that means that she can't be your closest friend. You still have a responsibility to love her and pray for her. That's best done from a distance.

Unfortunately, because of her mean condition, a confrontation is probably not the best thing, or at least shouldn't be done in the traditional way. Just refusing to let her control you anymore would be more effective. That means you start saying no when she tells you to do this or that. That means that you leave when she insults you or argues with you. Getting out of her way is usually the best option. But you also have to decide not to participate in her mean any longer. I'm just gonna guess here, but I bet that more than likely when she's mean to other girls, you stand beside her, either in quiet agreement or actively participating, and now that has to stop. And you stopping is a form of confrontation for the 24–7 frenemy. Over time, as you stop gossiping with her, siding with her, and doing whatever she asks, she'll start to get the point.

BREAKING UP WITH THE 24-7 FRENEMY

Because of the 24–7 frenemy's hot temper, breaking up with her is more than likely best to do gradually. Just like your confrontation can't be as direct as with other frenemies, so your breakup would be more than likely best done gently. Gradually decrease the time you spend with her by saying you're busy when she asks you to go somewhere or when she starts an on-line conversation. Saying no to a frenemy can be really hard, but you have to look at saying no as your safest way of getting her out of your life.

If you aren't afraid of her reactions and are willing to make a stand, then you can most certainly break up the old-fashioned way by telling her you don't want to hang out with her anymore. Just be prepared for her wrath. More than likely she's going to go down swinging. She might even insult you, attack you, and even smear you. And you need to be ready to handle all that involves.

When you decide you're ready to break up with her, you have to be strong. You have spent a lot of time obeying her, or at the very least fearing her, so saying no to her will be unusual for you. But you have to be firm. You can't give in to her pleadings or her manipulations. Instead, you have to keep in mind why you are walking away.

Breaking up is never fun. It hurts, and I wish it never had to happen, but sometimes it does. You can't keep bowing at the feet of your frenemy. If you've done all you can to change the way you react to her, to confront her sin, and to love and pray for her and you still don't see any change, then you can't feel guilty about walking away from your frenemyship.

People don't like being rejected, especially not mean people. So you can't expect this process to be easy, but easy isn't what you signed up for when you became a believer. People say that anything that doesn't kill you only makes you stronger, and that is really true in this case. Her words, her actions—none of it can separate you from the love of God. (Romans 8:38-39) You have all you need inside of you to stand up to her and to refuse to let her lead you down a bad path. So be brave, my friend, and stop being the victim. Remember that God's way is the best way, and his way is always loving and kind. And if you need more help dealing with Mean Girls, pick up the book *Mean Girls: Facing Your Beauty Turned Beast*. You always have to put love first and self second, but never ever let yourself put her above all.

> Christ has freed us so that we may enjoy the benefits of freedom. Therefore, be firm [in this freedom], and don't become slaves again.
>
> Galatians 5:1

The Frenemy
You Can't Leave

There is a frenemy you can never break up with. This frenemy is the one who is a permanent or semi-permanent part of your life. If you live with your frenemy or are just related to a frenemy who you can never truly walk away from, you need to learn the best way of dealing with the broken relationship so that you can survive the time of testing you are going through right now as you interact with them on a regular basis. Everything you've read up to the "Breaking Up" chapter of this book is useful for the frenemy that never goes away, so I hope that you have tried all the things I've already talked about. Now, if things still haven't improved, there are still a few more things you can try in order to rearrange your life so that hopefully you can find a little peace.

The most important thing in life with frenemies is that you do not allow them to lead you into sin. Your strength comes in knowing that there is something bigger than you, something bigger than this torture. The apostle Paul put it this way:

> We serve God whether people honor us or despise us, whether they slander us or praise us. We are honest, but they call us impostors. We are ignored, even though we are well known. We live close to death, but we are still alive. We have been beaten, but we have not been killed. Our hearts ache, but we always have joy. We are poor, but we give spiritual riches to others. We own nothing, and yet we have everything.
>
> 2 Corinthians 6:8–10 NLT

No matter what this frenemy does, she can never pull you away from your faith or your obedience to that faith.

But this relationship will be one of the hardest you've ever had to endure. Sometimes you will want to scream or lock yourself in your room and never come out again. The frenemy that you live with or are related to can feel like a tool in the hand of Satan himself. You might feel like she was sent just to destroy you, but chances are that is not the case. In this life, you are going to have a lot of relationships—friends, acquaintances, classmates, coworkers, family, and because you will have relationships, you are bound to have trials. Human interaction guarantees it. No one is perfect, so when two imperfect people come together, sin sees a great opportunity to join in the fun.

The most freedom you can find in difficult relationships is in your faith that nothing and no one can tear you from the hand of God (see Romans 8:39 again). If you

The Frenemy You Can't Leave

think that God is sovereign, meaning he has everything under control, then you will be less controlled by the frenemy and more controlled by God. No matter how close your frenemy is, no matter if she sleeps under the same roof as you or shares the same bloodline, she's not as close to you as God himself. She can't control your will or your spirit, and because of that you can have hope. The attacks might never stop, but that doesn't mean you can't be free from their sting. Living with the frenemy that never goes away might just be your chance to strengthen your faith and empower your spirit to believe fully in the God you cannot see but whose Word you choose to believe. Right now it's your choice: you can either let the frenemy destroy you or let this experience strengthen you.

Do you ever lift weights? Did you know that lifting weights is hurting your muscles? Yep, it's tearing them apart from the strain, but no worries, that's the goal. Your muscles need to be torn a little so that they can rebuild into even bigger and better muscles. To your body, the act of lifting weights might not seem like a fun experience, but that's because your muscles don't know that the result is going to be more strength and growth. Well, the same is true for your spirit. The experiences you are having right now might feel like they are tearing you down, and they actually might be, but if you're willing to look up instead of out, you can take the pain and use it to grow and strengthen your mind, your emotions, and your spirit.

The truth is that in this relationship that you can't get out of anytime soon, you have two options: you can either let it destroy

Frenemies

you or let it make you stronger. The choice is yours and yours alone. I hope that you choose to get stronger; it's the smart choice. The other choice will only make your life miserable and weak and make the frenemy stronger and meaner. You have more control of your life than you might know. The frenemy might be relentless; she might be trying to make your life miserable, but she can never control your mind or your spirit. You have complete freedom and control within yourself—maybe not on the outside, with the things you are allowed or not allowed to do around her, but most definitely on the inside, you can be free to control yourself.

For several years of my life, on two separate occasions, I lived with my frenemies, and each time I was tormented by them. I was fearful and angry. I wanted to get out and away, but that wasn't going to happen anytime soon. We lived in the same house, so I had to find ways to make it work. So I know exactly what you are going through. I understand the sick feeling in the pit of your stomach that you get when walk in the door. I know the way you imagine retaliating or putting them in their place. I know the conversations you rehearse in your mind after you've had a fight with them. And I know that the relationship can be changed; it can improve. It's not always easy, but there is hope. So let me give you some practical ways that you can make your life better while in close proximity to your frenemy that won't go away.

Control Yourself

In your relationship with your family frenemy, self-control is your best friend. You can never control another person, but there are two people in this relationship. Can you imagine controlling 50 percent of the relationship? When you can control yourself around your frenemy, you do just that. You gain a significant amount of power when you just start to control yourself.

If you feel like your parent is your frenemy, then there are a few things to think about. A few years ago I wrote a book called *Stupid Parents: Why They Just Don't Understand and How You Can Help*. In the book, I talk to kids about how to change their relationship with their parents. My goal is to bring peace back to the family and to help kids and parents (I also wrote one for them called *Not-So-Stupid Parents*) learn to stop the fighting and start getting along, or at least peacefully coexisting. And the main thing I stress is that you first have to decide what you want in this relationship. If you want peace, or freedom from the mean, then good—at least you have a goal. Then you have to decide how get to that goal. In many cases, people in authority over you, like parents, will tell you what they want from you. They might even give you a list, and once you know what they want, your best way to get peace is to just do it. God's Word even has a payoff for this option. Look at this, *"Honor your father and your mother, so that you may live for a long time in the land the Lord your God is giving you."* (Exodus 20:12 GWT)

When you refuse to argue, roll your eyes, or walk away, and you decide to just do what they ask, even if it seems unfair, you honor your parents, and that helps you to learn to live with your frenemy parent. More than likely you aren't going to divorce yourself from your parents and so you've got to learn to live with them, frenemy or not.

Self-control is your friend. Each time you practice self-control, you get stronger. It doesn't matter how you do it; any act of self-control leads to more strength on your part. So learning to practice self-control in dealing with your frenemy should be your number one goal. No matter if they're your parents or not, your biggest strength lies in your ability to control yourself. When you lose control and get angry or depressed, you effectively give control of your life over to someone else. That is idolatry—creating a little god out of your frenemy. Stop that today. Don't let the pain they inflict control you, but choose to be controlled by love himself: the God who knows all, sees all, and can handle all.

Self-control, as it relates to a frenemy you live with, means that you start to live with the big picture in mind, and that you stop worrying about the small stuff. I know it might not seem small right now, but in comparison to what God has in store, it's small beans. So learn self-control, pray for it, practice it. Don't let her emotions or words get you off track. Just like a frenemy you don't live with, you have to decide what's more important: their meanness or your faithfulness.

Don't Relive Their Mean

When someone makes me mad and I walk away from them, I love to rehearse what I should have said to them, over and over again. I find some kind of sick pleasure in thinking about what they said or did and going over it again and again, proving them wrong in my mind or in the privacy of my own room. On some level it feels good, and I suppose I work through it, but when I relive the memory, I also make it worse. I have discovered that reliving mean is the best way to get your heart rate up. It only prolongs the fight. It's picking at the wound, and it gives the frenemy more of your strength and more of your emotions.

When I told myself that I wouldn't let their mess become my mess and chose to not relive what they said but just walk away and move on, I found that my problems with them were less of a problem, and believe it or not, our relationship got better. I think a lot of it had to do with the fact that I wasn't holding onto any resentment and I wasn't retaliating in any way, but was just moving on.

It's super hard to get this, but it is a fact of life: you are 50 percent of the equation. And that means you have at least 50 percent of the power to make the relationship better. Those are pretty good odds, certainly better than believing you are 100 percent helpless in the situation. So to gain control and stop letting her get into your very soul, stop reliving the last fight you had with her. Don't go over and over again in your mind how mean she is or how wrong she is. Do the opposite—do something else, get your mind busy and change the subject. The longer you hold on to her sin, the longer her sin hurts you. So let it go and let it be gone.

Part of Jesus's call to us to "turn the other cheek" (see Matthew 5:39) is refusing to fight back mentally. In other words, as you think about the situation, decide to let her slap be the last. Don't think any further about what she did or said or what you wish you would have said or done. You have to remember that more is at stake here than just your emotions. You are responsible for

Frenemies

your thoughts. So when you think hateful angry thoughts, look out—God's Word makes it pretty clear that this is a dangerous practice: "But I say, if you are even angry with someone, you are subject to judgment! If you call someone an idiot, you are in danger of being brought before the court. And if you curse someone, you are in danger of the fires of hell" (Matthew 5:22 NLT). The reason is that you are held just as guilty for your thoughts as you are for your actions (see Matthew 5:28).

So don't let her actions and your mental reactions be a cause for your sin. You have to refuse to let her continue to hurt you even when she isn't near you. Change the subject in your mind as quickly as you can. If that seems too hard, then open up your Bible, turn on some worship music, and run to God. He will help you to overcome her mean. I promise you that when you do this, you will weaken the hold of your frenemy on your heart.

Practice Love

With your family frenemy, breaking up isn't an option, so you've got to work even harder just to find some peace. In family relationships (even in temporary families, like roommates) you need a little extra love. Loving means letting go of your thoughts of how things oughta be. You like things done a certain way, and when there's someone else living with you, it isn't always going to work that way, but even so you can't let that take away your desire or ability to love God's way. Love doesn't prove itself when loving is easy (see Matthew 5:46–48). Love proves itself when times are tough, when those you are loving aren't loving you back. Love in the hard times, in the attacks, in the face of disrespect is the truest kind of love.

Jesus is crazy about love—not the getting it but the giving it. It's easy, being human, for you to get stuck on the getting of love and to refuse to give unless you get, but that would make you like the unbeliever who gives only to get. When you practice love because God commands it, your burden is lifted. That happens because your focus is off the kindness or love (or lack thereof) of the other person and on the kindness and love of God. You love because of his great love for you, not because of what the frenemy does or doesn't do. This kind of love frees you because resentment and hate, the alternatives, trap you. They weaken you and draw you inward into misery. When your focus is on your pain, your pain is magnified, but when your focus is on obeying God's commands, your strength is magnified instead.

So how do you practice love with your family frenemy? First of all, you refuse to fight. Love doesn't hit back. It doesn't get revenge; it doesn't keep a record of what the other person is doing wrong. It isn't about me, me, me, but about God. Here are some pretty basic things to consider when it comes to love:

Don't roll your eyes when they talk.
Don't walk away while they are talking.
Don't try to out-shout them.
Never use the words *stupid* or *hate*.

Frenemies

Don't frown whenever you see them.

Don't look for the worst in them.

Don't be disrespectful.

And here are some things to do in order to love them:

Look for the good things in them.

Smile when you see them.

Look them in the eyes.

Respect them.

Try to see things from their perspective.

Pray for them.

Figure out what triggers their mean and try to avoid it.

Love isn't easy; it wasn't meant to be. It isn't about feeling good or loved in return. Jesus didn't feel good as he hung on the cross, but that didn't make him get down and walk away. He knew the power of love was all that could save humanity. And that's why love never gives up being loving. It has to stand even in the face of torture. Your love might never be returned here on earth, but your heart will be pulled closer and closer to God as you love. Obedience to his Word and his command to love even the worst of people (see Romans 12:14) will lead you to hope, healing, and happiness.

Accept Sanctification

Sanctification is a big word for the process of becoming holy. It starts as soon as you accept Christ, and it goes on until you join him in heaven. But it can be a rough and difficult road. The perfecting of your soul takes work. Like building muscles, sanctification means heavy lifting and dedication. The process of sanctification is best accomplished in the hard times. When you are tested, broken, and weakened, then you are given the chance to build up not yourself but your faith in the one who rescues you.

The author James MacDonald once said something that completely changed the way I think about frenemies: "God's goal is not to make you happy; it's to make you holy." Holiness is far more beneficial than happiness. And maybe, just maybe, this frenemy that you can't get rid of will be the tool of sanctification that your life needs. But it will only be that way if you let it be. That means that each time you are attacked or hurt by your frenemy, instead of whining or hating, complaining or worrying, you look inside and see what God wants you to learn about yourself in this moment. Does something in you need to be purified? Do you have a part of you that is pulling you away from God and needs to be rooted out?

Sometimes difficult people can give you good insight into the sinful and weak areas of your life. The best way to use their sin and their mean is to let it show you more about who God is and who He wants you to be—not to make it about the pain or the hurt, but to make it about the sanctification of your soul. There is power in using their attacks to reveal the areas in your life where you need forgiveness and where you need to draw closer to God.

Don't let the opportunity of living with your frenemy go to waste. Use each encounter, each thing they do, to teach you things about yourself and mostly about your God. What does he call you to do in difficult situations? Do those things. What does he ask of you when the world attacks? Now's your chance to do it. Find out what pleases God and make that a part of your response. This is gonna require some work, some research, some prayer, and some effort on your part, but all of this work only makes you stronger. It draws you closer to God and gives you more insight into yourself and your relationship with the Creator.

I can remember one time when my frenemy got mad at me for something she thought was "stupid" about how I communicated with people. She went off on me, and by the end I was so angry I just stormed off. The only thing I could do was go to my room and cry to God. And so I did. But as I cried and as I listened, he started to work on me. I brought what she said to him and opened up his Word, and I saw that although her way of talking to me wasn't kind, what she was saying had some truth to it. So I took the pieces of truth I saw and made them a part of my life.

Pride says, "I am perfect and she is wrong." But humility says, "Where can I change, Lord?" In humility, you can find the strength to rise above the insults and the attacks and instead to use them for good. Is there any truth at all to what your frenemy says? If you can find any, then thank God and thank her. Ask forgiveness from her and thank her for pointing out your weakness. Not only will she be shocked, but it will soften her.

And finally, pray for her. Pray that she will hear from God and ask that even if she doesn't, then at the very least he will use her mightily in your life. Throughout history, God has used bad people to accomplish his goals (see Romans 9:17–18). He assigns people to be a thorn in your flesh (see 2 Corinthians 12:7). And you can

Living with a Violent Frenemy

If your frenemy is abusive or violent, you should never just accept their aggression in the name of love. In those situations, things have gotten out of hand and something needs to be done. If you live in a violent home, you have to report it. Talk to a counselor, a teacher, a pastor, or even the police. You don't glorify God by taking abuse as punishment or considering it your payment in life. If you can't move away from the violent frenemy, then you have to report them, for their own good, before they do something that would endanger not only your life but theirs as well.

either run from those messengers sent to reveal your weakness to you, or argue with them and refuse their message.

When you live with a frenemy, you have to continually keep going to God. You need to keep talking to him about the situation and most of all listening to him. Where is he in this? Why has he allowed it in your life? What will he make out of you through this situation? You can find answers to all these questions in the presence of God. Believe it, and believe him when he says, "I know the plans I have for you . . . plans to prosper you and not to harm you, plans to give you hope and a future" (Jeremiah 29:11 NIV).

Tune Them Out

In some situations, the only thing that will work with your frenemy is to just tune them out. That doesn't mean you ignore

them but that you change the frequency on which you listen
to them. To tune out someone properly, you have to listen to
them not on a human level but on a heavenly level. In other
words, look at them through God's eyes, taking into consider-
ation their spiritual and emotional weaknesses. It's not exactly
reading between the lines, but it's listening with a God
filter on, knowing that God loves her as much as he
loves you and that he wants you to love her too.
This is kind of like putting on the armor of God to
protect yourself so that you don't get hit by all her
little jabs and pricks. You still see her, you still love
her, but you don't react to all the arrows she shoots your
way because you are concentrating on who God is and who
you are because of him.

The armor of God is a good place to start when it comes to
tuning out. I have found it a really good practice to ask God each
morning to suit me up in his armor. I pray something like this:

> Dear God, please put your armor on me this morning to
> protect me from the attacks that I know are gonna come
> at me. Put on the helmet of salvation to protect my mind
> from the things I will see and hear. Put the breastplate of
> righteousness on my chest so that I can remember that I
> already have a righteousness that doesn't come from who
> I am or what I've done but comes from who you are and
> what you've done. Wrap the belt of truth around my waist
> so that I will be protected by the truth and always remem-
> ber it, even when I am told the opposite. Put the shield
> of faith into my hand so I can resist the enemy and so
> that I can deflect any attacks with the knowledge that
> you are all I need and that nothing can separate me
> from your love. And on my feet put the sandals of
> the gospel of peace. May I always remember what
> really matters and always speak of Jesus's death

and resurrection. Help me to promote and live in peace. And finally, give me the sword of the Spirit in my hand so that I can defend myself with your truth when the attacks come. May I never use it as an offensive weapon but only to defend and protect. Amen.

Every day that I put on the armor of God, I am protected. I am suited up and ready for whatever might come my way. Tune your frenemies out today by preparing for battle God's way. When you do, you will learn to ignore the unimportant and to refuse to react to the mean. Always be respectful and loving, but don't let your heart tune in to their anger or bitterness. Hear only what you need to hear in order to be kind, and let the other stuff bounce off your armor.

Identify with Jesus

Finally, when you've done everything you can to stand on faith and obedience, you have to remember that you aren't alone. Millions of others around the world are going through the same exact things you are going through. In fact, you have a God who knows exactly what you are going through because he went through his own suffering while he walked this earth. Always remember that your goal as a believer is to become more like Christ, and so it shouldn't surprise you when you suffer. "God called you to endure suffering because Christ suffered for you. He left you an example so that you could follow in his footsteps" (1 Peter 2:21).

Don't run away from suffering like it's something terrible and pointless. It might be painful and yucky, but it is never pointless

Frenemies

if you're willing to let it do its work. Suffering purifies you. It teaches you a lot about yourself and about your God if you are willing to listen, but it takes work. The easy way to deal with suffering is to escape it, avoid it, steer clear of it. But the best way to deal with suffering is to confront it head-on and to let it shine a light on your life, reminding your heart that all you need is God—not acceptance or peace, not respect or adoration. Though those things are amazing, they aren't required for your soul. But holiness is. And holiness can be yours if you are willing to accept it (see 1 Thessalonians 4:7; Hebrews 12:14).

Suffering is essential in the life of a believer. Without suffering, there would be no salvation, because the horrific suffering of Christ is the only way we can be saved at all (see Hebrews 2:10). Out of suffering comes the most amazing thing ever: reconciliation with God, a making things right between you. Suffering isn't as horrible as it seems. It has a purpose and a payoff, but you have to look beyond the pain to the plan. As you suffer, I pray that you won't concentrate on the perpetrator of the pain but on the face of God. Like Jesus did when he suffered, pray for the ones who hurt you (see Luke 23:34) and stand on the knowledge that something far greater awaits you.

Let the frenemy that you can't leave be used by God to draw you to him. If you can't get away from your family frenemy, then you have to find the hand of God in your life. You have to trust that he is in control and that he never gives you more than you can handle (see 1 Corinthians 10:13). When you really trust God and take him at his word, you know that this suffering you are going through right now is nothing compared

The Frenemy You Can't Leave

to how amazing life will be on the other side, in heaven (see Romans 8:18). You know that no one can kill you unless God let's them. And you know that what doesn't kill you only makes you stronger.

Your role in this process is one of focus protection. You have to protect your focus and refuse to look at anything in your life as something out of God's control or out of his will. Whether he allows it because he gave human beings free will, or because it's something he wants specifically for your life, you have to trust that God is in control. You might feel like a battle is raging against you, but if you can take your eyes off the battle and put them onto the one who is above all, you will find a way of peace.

If you become seasick on a boat in the middle of the ocean, the best way to stop the sickness is to fix your eyes on the horizon. The consistency of the unmovable line where the water meets the sky helps your sickened stomach to get some rest from the continual rocking and rhythm of the pounding sea. Think of God as the horizon that you have to focus on. Even though the waves crash in around you, and the water sprays you and the salt burns, the horizon stays steady. Don't think anything in your life is a thing that God can't make something good out of or that he can't and won't use to transform your life and to make you more holy.

Blaming your circumstance on anyone else is always a position of weakness, but accepting it as allowed by God for your greater good empowers you to seek the truth, to seek his face, and to find out what amazing glory he wants to bring through this present suffering. If you want freedom from the frenemy

that you can't leave, then you have to consider her presence in your life as a tool in the hand of God. Refuse to complain (see Philippians 2:14), refuse to hate (see 1 John 2:11), and refuse to worry (see Matthew 6:25–27; 1 Peter 5:7), but choose to trust (see Psalm 28:7) and to believe (see Hebrews 11:1). When you do, you'll find your heart set free to soar above on wings like eagles (see Isaiah 40:31). Freedom exists in your heart and in your mind. Make the focus of your life God's truth and his Word, and you'll be set free from the worry and the fear. Trust him! He will never leave you or forsake you (see Hebrews 13:5).

> **See how good and pleasant it is when brothers and sisters live together in harmony!**
>
> Psalm 133:1

One Final Thing

The most power you can have in your life comes from looking at everything from the perspective of faith. How can this or that help my faith, make it stronger, draw me closer to God? When you can make everything about him instead of about you, you will find a freedom and a strength you've never known. You can be set free from the battles of life when you see everything in the light of God's hand on your life like the hand of a potter on

his creation. <u>God is</u> called <u>the potter</u> for a reason (see Isaiah 29:16;). He designed you, and he's making you into the vessel (pot) that he wants you to become. You can either fight the potter's wheel as it throws you around and his hand as he molds you and shapes you, or you can let him mold you and make you smooth and perfect. It hurts to be molded, it hurts to be changed, but change will make you whole. It will improve your heart and your mind, and maybe even your relationship with your frenemy.

Know that your fight isn't really against your frenemy. She's not really the enemy here. All battles that you face with humans on earth are ultimately spiritual battles. And though they might be against an unholy enemy, they might very well also be against sin—the sin in the life of others and the sin in your own life. Just never look at anything as unrelated to things of the spirit. Everything that happens to you and around you has some spiritual value, be it negative or positive. In other words, this battle isn't against a girl but is against sin and its hold on the world (see Ephesians 6:12). If you can look at everything from this spiritual perspective, you can operate under battle conditions more powerfully. When you think your enemy is in one place and they are really in another, you can't be effective. But when you realize where the true battle is, you can draw on all the weapons you need for that battle.

So I encourage you to focus on things of the Spirit every day before you walk out of the house. Turn to God and ask him to suit you up in his armor (see Ephesians 6:11–17). As you ask him for each thing, remind yourself of what these pieces will do for you. The helmet will protect you from the slings and arrows of the enemy that fly through the air in an attempt to wound you. The breastplate of righteousness is there to cover you with the righteousness that comes not from your power but from Christ's. The belt of truth is there to remind you of everything that God has shown you and will show you. The sandals of the gospel of peace represent the power of the life and death of Jesus Christ and the peace you can offer to others as you share it. And the great sword of the Spirit is God's Word itself, the Bible. With it you can fight any attack of the enemy. It is a defensive weapon, used to protect yourself and others. And you need to hold it tightly in your hand every day.

Be prepared for the battle that will rage as you face your frenemy head-on spiritually. But know that as you do, God will be with you if you will be with him. Don't ever let his Word be too far from your heart. Read it, write it, memorize it. Learn what God has to say about the sin in your life and the sin in your friend's life. Be prepared for the battle. Don't take your eyes off him, but look at everything from his viewpoint.

Finally, know that this too shall pass. Right now it might look like things will never get better, never progress, but everything changes, especially when given over to the hand of God. Things are always changing, life is never stagnant for one who believes God is in everything. One day, your frenemy relationship may be something you talk about in order to help other girls with the same kinds of problems, so learn as you go. Take notes; write in journals; keep verses handy while committing them to memory. Even jump online and go to Hungry Planet's online social network, iFuse.com, where you can chat up with other girls going through the same thing and even ask me questions about dealing with your frenemy.

Remember what you've learned here today and through this process, and be ready to share it and teach it to others. Nothing is hopeless and nothing is useless in the life of a believer who trusts the God she believes in. Live up to your name—you are a believer, not a doubter! Be brave, strong, and courageous. Love deeply and be holy! One day soon all this misery will end. But through it all, continue to learn the art and discipline of loving God and loving others from the one who loves perfectly, Jesus.

Hayley

*H*ayley DiMarco is founder of Hungry Planet, a company that creates cutting-edge books to connect with the multitasking mind-set. Hungry Planet is where she writes, co-writes, or edits all of the company's content for teens and former teens. She has written or co-written numerous bestselling and award-winning books, including *Dateable*, *Mean Girls*, *Sexy Girls*, *Technical Virgin*, *B4UD8,* and *The Woman of Mystery*. Hayley lives with her husband and daughter in Nashville, Tennessee.

You can find Hayley at www.ifuse.com and her books at www.hungryplanet.net

Hungry Planet Helps Teens Become

When you become a God Girl, your life
will never be the same.

 Revell
a division of Baker Publishing Group
www.RevellBooks.com

Available Wherever Books Are Sold

the People God Meant Them to Be

Becoming a God Guy can change
your life for the better.

Hungry
Planet

www.hungryplanet.net

<iFuse>
life + faith + love + truth

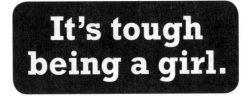

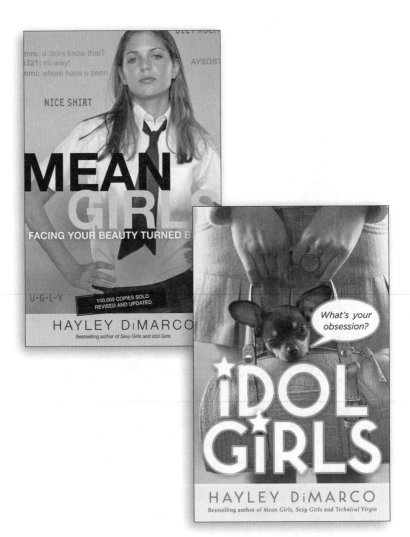

But Hayley can help.

SEXY GIRLS
How Hot Is Too Hot

HAYLEY DiMARCO
BESTSELLING AUTHOR OF *MEAN GIRLS* AND *DATEABLE*

TECHNICAL
Virgin
HOW FAR IS TOO FAR?

A *SEXY GIRLS* BOOK

HAYLEY DiMARCO
BESTSELLING AUTHOR OF *MEAN GIRLS* AND *DATEABLE*

Find the advice
you need in these
bestselling books!

Dating or waiting?
First date or 500th?

Hungry Planet tells you everything you need to know.

Available wherever books are sold.

Now Available in Paperback
Lead your group through the whole PB&J series

Use these great resources to get your crew excited:

- **iFuse.com**: sign up your group in the new social community from HP!
- **HungryPlanet.tv**: download videos of Hayley introducing each section of the PB&J series
- **HungryPlanet.net**: download free leader's guides

For case quantity discounts of **30–50% off** the regular retail price for your church or group, please visit www.direct2church.com or email us at Direct2Church@BakerPublishingGroup.com.

Revell
a division of Baker Publishing Group
www.RevellBooks.com

Hungry Planet
www.hungryplanet.net

<iFuse> beta
life + faith + love + truth

life + faith + love + truth

| Main | Invite | My Page | Members | Groups | Forum |

Page   Friends   Blog

Hayley DiMarco's Page

Hayley DiMarco

Female

Nashville, TN, United States

+ Add as friend

✉ Send a Message

⅄ Share

Latest Activity

Hayley DiMarco left a comment for Brittany
1 day ago

Erin left a comment for Hayley DiMarco
1 day ago

Taylor and Hayley DiMarco are now friends

1 day ago

Hayley DiMarco added the blog post 'Sexy Fashion Fixes'
1 day ago

Hayley DiMarco left a comment for Erin
1 day ago

Hayley DiMarco left a comment for Katie
1 day ago

Hayley DiMarco is chief creative officer and founder of Hungry Planet, where she writes and creates cutting-edge books that connect with the multitasking mind-set. She has written and co-written numerous bestselling books for both teens and adults, including *Dateable*, *Mean Girls*, *Sexy Girls*, and *Technical Virgin*. She and her husband, Michael, live in Nashville, Tennessee.

Revell
a division of Baker Publishing Group
www.RevellBooks.com

www.hungryplanet.net

life + faith + love + truth